1000 Columbo Facts

Second Edition

Phillip Allan

Contents

Introduction

Columbo is an iconic police procedural show which ran from 1968 to 2003. The show was very popular during its run, especially in the 1970s and remains very popular today throughout the world.

The show has a wonderful performance by Peter Falk as the disheveled, eccentric but extremely able detective. The world depicted is colourful and often surreal with Columbo chasing murderers who are often rich and highly intelligent. Columbo has high production values, great writing, wonderful guest stars and many famous personalities involved in production.

Find out more about the world of Columbo with this book with information on the cast and crew, anecdotes, episodes, characters, locations, mistakes and other fascinating Columbo facts in this book.

The Facts

(1) Columbo began life in 1968 as a television film called Prescription: Murder - which aired on February 20th 1968.

(2) Gene Barry, who played the villain (Dr. Ray Flemming) in Prescription: Murder, was in a great many things but one of his early roles was as the bespectacled square-jawed physicist Dr Clayton Forrester in the 1953 film The War of the Worlds. The film was the first screen adaption of the classic HG Wells novel and won an Oscar for its colourful and striking special effects.

(3) Peter Falk was diagnosed with eye cancer when he was three and had to have an eye removed. When he later became an actor he was told more than once that his glass eye would probably rule out any film work (a studio boss once heartlessly commented that he could get an actor with two eyes for the same money) but Peter Falk had the last laugh, being nominated for an Oscar for Murder Incorporated, the first film he ever made. The Columbo episode A Trace of Murder is the first to acknowledge that Columbo - like Peter Falk - has one eye. At a crime scene with a colleague, Columbo comments that 'three eyes' are better than one.

(4) Richard Levinson and William Link said the detective character Porfiry Petrovich in Crime and Punishment was an influence on Columbo. Published in 1886 and written by Fyodor Dostoevsky, Crime and Punishment is about a former student named Rodion Raskolnikov who is suffering from severe financial problems and ends up murdering a pawnbroker to rectify his money worries. Raskolnikov had rationalised the murder by telling himself that the pawnbroker was a bad person anyway and that with money he could now live a much better life and do some good with

his new found wealth. He could, for example, help his family and save his sister from an unhappy marriage. However, Raskolnikov learns that murder and taking a life is not quite this simple.

After the act is done and Raskolnikov has killed, he is wracked with guilt and disgust for his actions. His life and mental state soon begins to frazzle and descend into paranoia and confusion. Because of his extreme guilt, he finds that he can't enjoy the money he has stolen because it was not acquired through honest means. Although the world is apparently no poorer for lacking a heartless pawnbroker, Raskolnikov discovers that a criminal act as serious as murder preys on the mind and makes it impossible for him to move on with his life. He soon begins to have an urge to confess - the only way to clear his soul.

(5) Theodore Bikel, who played Oliver Brandt in The Bye-Bye Sky High I.Q. Murder Case, unsuccessfully tested for the part of the villain Auric Goldfinger in the classic James Bond film Goldfinger. It was obviously Gert Frobe who got this part in the end. They had to dub Frobe though because his English wasn't great.

(6) Columbo is an Italian-American and very proud of his Italian roots. In real life though Peter Falk's parents and ancestors were from eastern Europe and he did not have any Italian ancestry.

(7) Stephen Caffrey, who played the student Justin Rowe in Columbo Goes to College, was 31 years-old at the time. He was a youthful looking 31 though so just about got away with it.

(8) Nicholas Colasanto, who directed the Columbo episodes Étude in Black and Swan Song, later became a familiar face on

television for his role as the absent minded bartender Coach in the sitcom Cheers.

(9) In the story Mind Over Mayhem, the boy genius is called Stephen Spelberg. This is a tribute by episode writers Steven Bochco and Dean Hargrove to Steven Spielberg - who directed Murder by the Book in 1971. Alex Brady, the young genius film director in the 1989 Columbo episode Murder, Smoke and Shadows seems (the murder part aside obviously) somewhat inspired by Steven Spielberg - which is slightly odd given that Brady is the villain!

(10) In the episode Agenda for Murder a piece of evidence implicating the murderer involves a bitemark on a piece of cheese. Columbo references Ted Bundy when it comes to the cheese and says that Bundy's teeth were a factor in his conviction for his murderous attack on a college dorm in Florida. This is true.

The two most crucial pieces of evidence that sealed the fate of Bundy were (in order of importance) eyewitness Nita Neary identifying Ted Bundy in court as the man she saw leaving the Chi Omega house as she arrived home on the night of the murders and Bundy's teeth (Bundy had been understandably reluctant to allow his teeth to be photographed but ultimately had no say in the matter) proving to be an exact match for the bite marks on Chi Omega victim Lisa Levy's left buttock. It was the teeth marks that proved vital in convicting Bundy and establishing his guilt.

The dentist Dr. Richard Souviron was able to show in court that blow-ups of Bundy's teeth matched the injury on Levy's buttock. There was a chip in one of Bundy's front teeth which made it easier to match him to the injury on the victim. Bundy, who had obviously deduced that this evidence was a disaster for his case, tried to maintain that the chip in his tooth had occurred after the Chi Omega attacks and his defence team tried to fog the evidence by suggesting that this sort of thing wasn't an exact science and the dentist was speculating rather than asserting a fact. Souviron stuck to his guns though. He insisted that he was completely certain that Bundy's teeth matched the bite marks. While Bundy's teeth were a factor in one of his convictions it is probably more questionable whether one could actually be convicted for murder on the basis of a tiny half nibbled piece of cheese!

(11) The only episodes of Columbo on IMDB with a rating under 7 (out of ten) are Last Salute to the Commodore, No Time to Die, Murder in Malibu, A Matter of Honor, Murder with Too Many notes, Grand Deceptions, Dead Weight and Undercover.

(12) Last Salute to the Commodore is the lowest rated episode of Columbo on IMDB with a (at the time of writing) score of 6.2 out of 10. Last Salute to the Commodore is certainly what you might describe as an acquired taste. The episode did have its fans (Peter Falk among them) but for others this surreal episode (in which an amused and spaced out Columbo appears to be drunk or high for much of the story) felt rather too much like a joke that the director Patrick McGoohan and Peter Falk were in on but the audience were not.

(13) Patrick McGoohan was best known for creating and starring in the surreal British television classic The Prisoner. The Prisoner only ran for seventeen episodes from 1967 to 1968 but its surreal atmosphere and location (the Hotel Portmeirion in Penrhyndeudraeth, North Wales), not to mention the tightly wound, irritable and defiant central character 'Number Six', marvelously played by Patrick McGoohan, was enough to give it enduring cult status and a

reputation as one of the most interesting fantasy shows ever to appear on television. Number Six was an unnamed British agent of some sort who resigns from his job only to wake up in a strange seaside village that seems to be impossible to escape from, is populated by eccentric characters, and closely watched over by surveillance devices.

(14) In the episode A Case of Immunity, Columbo is investigating the chief diplomat of the Legation of Suari. The Kingdom of Sauri is a fictional country created for the episode.

(15) Columbo never uses the police siren for his car. When he does have to dig it out he isn't even sure how it works.

(16) In the episode Now You See Him, the line 'Now is the time for all good men to come to the aid of the party...' is typed by Sgt. Wilson to test the typewriter. This line was a common one as part of practice for typing classes - which explains why Wilson types it. Charles E Weller was the person who created this 'typewriter drill' exercise.

(17) Lee Montgomery, who played the boy genius Stephen Spelberg in Mind Over Mayhem, later appeared in shows like Kojak, Fame and Highway to Heaven. His last acting credit is in 1987. Perhaps his finest hour came in the segment 'Bobby' of the 1977 Dan Curtis horror anthology television film Dead of Night. Montgomery played a little boy who is brought back to life by black magic.

(18) Clive Revill's character in The Conspirators in supposed to be from Belfast in Northern Ireland, but Revill is clearly attempting to do a southern Irish accent based on someone from the Republic of Ireland.

(19) In the episode Publish or Perish, the snooty waiter at Chasen's Restaurant is perplexed when Columbo orders some chilli. This was a little in-joke because in reality Chasen's was famed for doing good chilli.

(20) The young King Hamid Kamal of Suari in the episode A Case of Immunity was played by Barry Robins - who (as his name gives away) was not Arabic in real life. Robins appeared in musicals on the stage and was probably best known for the film Bless the Beasts and Children. His last acting credit was in 1978 and he sadly died of complications from AIDS in 1986.

(21) In the episode Publish or Perish, Columbo reveals that he and his wife enjoy Bette Davis movies and sometimes have to watch them at 2 in the morning. You were at the mercy of television schedules in those days because there was no streaming and VCR's were not yet a common thing. Sian Barbara Allen played Shirley Blaine in the 1973 Columbo episode Lovely but Lethal. That same year Sian Barbara Allen starred in a film with Bette Davis - the made for television horror/mystery thriller Scream, Pretty Peggy.

(22) Columbo Likes the Nightlife featured Steve Schirripa as the mob connected character 'Freddie' who is following the case. When this last Columbo story was made, Steve Schirripa was also playing Bobby Baccalieri in the classic mafia series The Sopranos.

(23) Lou Nova has an uncredited part as a detective in Étude in Black. Nova was a former boxer who once fought the great Joe Louis for the world heavyweight championship. He took up acting after his retirement from the sweet science and appeared in a number of films and TV shows.

(24) The model of car Columbo drives is a 1959 Peugeot 403

Cabriolet convertible. Columbo is very proud of his car and seems to consider it to be a highly prized antique model but most of the characters he meets are not quite so impressed. Peter Falk chose his iconic Columbo car from a selection of old cars on the NBC studio lot. The car did not have an engine so needed work done.

(25) Milo Janus, the exercise fitness expert villain in An Exercise in Fatality, is said to be loosely based on Jack LaLanne. LaLanne was a fitness and nutritional expert and motivational speaker with his own television show. He wrote many books. In 1936 he opened one of America's first gym and health clubs. Jack LaLanne lived to be 96 and was still working out the day he died.

(26) Many of the villains in Columbo accept their fate with equanimity when the detective proves their guilt; but a notable exception to this is Dale Kingston in Suitable for Framing. Dale has a meltdown and desperately tries to talk his way out of the situation - despite the fact it is hopeless.

(27) Mrs. Columbo was an NBC television series launched in 1979 which - as the title implies - was supposed to about Columbo's wife Kate. Kate Columbo (played by Kate Mulgrew) is a reporter who solves crimes and has a daughter. At the time Columbo had just finished so NBC thought it might be a good idea to do a spin-off. Peter Falk (who obviously had nothing to do with this show) thought it was a terrible idea. Mrs. Columbo was not a success and quickly rowed back on the 'Columbo's wife' angle and dropped it altogether. It was also called Kate Columbo, Kate the Detective, and Kate Loves a Mystery and the character's name was eventually changed from Kate Columbo to Kate Callahan.

The initial idea that this was Columbo's wife was rather odd given that Kate Mulgrew was only in her early twenties at the time and nearly 30 years younger than Peter Falk. Mrs. Columbo was axed in 1980 and seems to be rather forgotten these days - save for its fleeting and strange connection to Columbo.

(28) Jackie Cooper stars as the murderer Nelson Hayward in Candidate for Crime. Jackie Cooper was a former child star whose career stretched from 1929 to 1987. You may know him as Clark Kent's boss at the Daily Planet in the Christopher Reeve Superman films. In his memoir, Jackie Cooper said that when he was a child star a director once got him to cry in a scene by threatening to shoot his dog. Cooper seemed to have some regret over his years as a child actor and believed they cost him a normal childhood.

(29) Peter Falk added Columbo's cigar habit. Peter Falk said the cigars Columbo smoked were literally just a pack of the cheapest ones in the store. Columbo is occasionally given or offered a high quality cigar by one of the urbane villains he is pestering. What he usually does on these occasions is say that he will save the cigar for later or a special occasion.

(30) Peter Falk said in an interview that he got a kick out of watching Columbo dubbed into other languages for foreign television.

(31) Peter Falk was quite late into acting after only doing it in his spare time while he had a 'normal' job, which, by all accounts, was rather dull and not something he was very well equipped to do. He was a management analyst with the Connecticut State Budget Bureau and said the tone was set when he arrived for his first day and got lost, ending up in the wrong building.

(32) Nicol Williamson stars as murderer Dr. Eric Mason in How To Dial A Murder. Nicol Williamson was a highly acclaimed British stage actor. His most famous role came a few years after his appearance in Columbo when he played Merlin in the John Boorman film Excalibur.

(33) In 1988 the co-creator of Columbo, William Link, thought that it was time to bring Columbo back as it had been off air since 1978. He successfully pitched the idea of a new Mystery Movie series including Columbo to the television network ABC. Columbo was resurrected in 1989 so you have two distinct eras of Columbo - the original 1970s era (Prescription: Murder notwithstanding) and the post 1989 'New' Columbo era with an older Peter Falk. It would probably be fair to say that some Columbo fans are a trifle sniffy about the post 1989 era and regard it as very inferior to the 1970s era. The 1970s Columbo set a very high standard that was almost impossible to replicate.

(34) Peter Falk was 61 years old when Columbo returned in 1989. Peter clearly has dyed hair as Columbo in the new episodes when the show came back. In the end he stopped doing this and allowed Columbo to have white and grey hair - which suited the character much more because Columbo is most assuredly not the sort of man who would dye his hair.

(35) Death Lends a Hand (1971) saw the first appearance of classic Columbo villain actor Robert Culp. Culp played the villain in three episodes - Death Lends a Hand, The Most Crucial Game, and Double Exposure. Many years later Culp also had a smaller role in Columbo Goes to College as the (unwitting) father of one of the killers. Robert Culp was a familiar face before Columbo in large part because of three memorable Outer Limits appearances (one could argue that Culp was rather like the Outer Limits version of that fantastic

Twilight Zone regular Jack Klugman).

Culp's major break though came with the television series I Spy. I Spy ran from 1965 to 1968. It starred Robert Culp as international tennis player Kelly Robinson with (the now disgraced) Bill Cosby as his trainer, Alexander Scott. In reality they were American spies, the sporting identities merely a cover. I Spy was a product of the spy crazed sixties when a slew of espionage films and television shows were inspired by the incredible success of the Cubby Broccoli/Harry Saltzman produced James Bond films. Culp and Cosby had an obvious rapport and the series was helped by some authentic location work in various exotic locales, from Europe to the Far East.

(36) The highest rated episode of 'New' Columbo on IMDB is a three way dead heat between Columbo Cries Wolf, Columbo Goes to College, and It's All in the Game. These three episodes have (at the time of writing) a score of 7.8 out of ten.

(37) Columbo was not originally intended to be a series. It was just supposed to be a movie of the week. Peter Falk turned the proposed Columbo series down a couple of times before he agreed to do it. His primary concern was to have a limited amount of episodes so that a high standard of scripts would be easier to maintain. Peter Falk was also understandably worried about a lengthy and constrictive television commitment which might preclude him from accepting film offers.

(38) Columbo's creators decided to not have Columbo frequently at police headquarters or at home when creating the series because they thought it was more effective if 'he drifted into our stories from limbo.' Columbo was shown at police headquarters on occasion but we never see his home - or his wife. In the 'New' Columbo episodes after 1989 we tend

to see Columbo at the police station somewhat more than we did in the original Columbo series.

(39) A culinary specialty of Columbo is a peanut butter and raisin sandwich. He makes this in Murder of a Rock Star and It's All in the Game.

(40) It is rare for the mild mannered Columbo to lose his cool and get angry but it has happened. Columbo gets angry in A Stitch in Crime when Leonard Nimoy's surgeon mocks him. Columbo also has a testy exchange in the hospital with Robert Conrad's Milo in An Exercise in Fatality. Columbo often gets on surprisingly well with the suspects he is investigating but there was certainly no love lost between the detective and Milo Janus.

(41) Katey Sagal had an early role in Columbo as a secretary in the episode Candidate for Crime. She was nineteen at the time. The episode was directed by her father Boris Sagal. Boris also directed another Columbo - The Greenhouse Jungle. Sadly, Boris Sagal died in a helicopter accident while directing the television miniseries World War III in 1982. Katey Sagal is best known for later playing Peggy Bundy in the sitcom Married... with Children.

(42) Columbo seems less scruffy and more neat and tidy in Prescription: Murder than his later appearances!

(43) Columbo's famous car is often depicted as as unreliable, dirty and in need of repairs. In reality this annoyed Peugeot as it showed their cars in a bad light!

(44) The episode Murder by the Book in 1971 was directed by Steven Spielberg - who was only about 24 at the time. Despite his tender age, Spielberg had already directed a segment on

Rod Serling's Night Gallery. Steven Spielberg is the youngest director to ever be given a contract by a major studio and is responsible for some of the highest grossing films of all time (Jaws, Raiders of the Lost Ark, E.T, Close Encounters of the Third Kind, Jurassic Park). Spielberg said that when he directed on television at the start of his career he treated every episode as a sort of audition to prove he could direct a feature film. The story about the young Spielberg just sneaking in uninvited at Universal Studios and moving into an empty office he found is a myth. The truth was less brazen and far more prosaic. Spielberg's father used his influence to get him a job as an editor at Universal and once he had his feet under the table (so to speak) it was obvious that he was remarkably talented for his age.

He firmly put himself on the map with the television film Duel and his first theatrical feature Sugarland Express but it was of course Jaws in 1975 that made Spielberg a hot ticket and in a position to do anything he wanted to.

(45) The mechanical shark from Jaws makes a cameo in the 1976 episode Fade in to Murder. This is a nice little reference to Steven Spielberg.

(46) The robot in Mind Over Mayhem is Robby the Robot. Robby the Robot was designed for the classic 1956 science fiction film Forbidden Planet. Robby the Robot made some appearances in The Twilight Zone and also numerous other shows too. Besides this famous robot, other actors from Forbidden Planet who appeared in Columbo were Anne Francis, Leslie Nielsen and Richard Anderson.

(47) Fisher Stevens is the youngest actor to be the main villain in Columbo. He was 25 years old when Murder, Smoke and Shadows came out.

(48) Caroline Treynor in The Bye-Bye Sky High I.Q. Murder Case is supposed to be fourteen. Carol Jones, who played the character, was actually 21 at the time.

(49) Double Exposure's plot relies on the effectiveness of subliminal cuts in films for advertising and Kepple mentions that the Consumer Trade Commission had banned such cuts. In reality, the use of such subliminal advertising has never been proven as effective and no such ban was made.

(50) William Christopher has a small part as a scientist in Mind Over Mayhem. Christopher was a familiar face on television for most of the seventies and the early 1980s for his role as Father Mulcahy in M*A*S*H.

(51) In the episode Try and Catch Me, when he giving his speech, Columbo says that despite his line of work (which unavoidably involves death and murder) his job does not depress him because he knows there are more nice people in the world than there are bad ones.

(52) 2003's Columbo Likes the Nightlife has a rave nightclub theme and modern soundtrack and drags Columbo into the 21st century. One could be forgiven for expecting this episode to be ill-advised but many rank it as one the better 'New' Columbo episodes.

(53) Columbo is fascinated by technology. He seems especially tickled by the (at the time still fairly new) concept of mobile phones in some of the 'New' Columbo episodes.

(54) Bing Crosby was first choice for the part of Columbo. He turned down the role as he thought it would take too long to film and he wanted to enjoy his later years and play golf. On the afternoon of October 14, 1977, Crosby was playing at the

La Morajela golf course near Madrid, Spain. After the 18th hole, Crosby started his walk back to the clubhouse and dropped dead from a massive heart attack. He was 74.

(55) Columbo says more than once in the series that he doesn't like blood. Despite this though Columbo never seems too phased or bothered by dead bodies at a crime scene. In the episode A Stitch in Crime we see that Columbo, despite being a homicide detective, IS very queasy and uncomfortable when he has a view of the surgery taking place at the hospital.

(56) Walter Koenig appears as as Sgt. Johnson in Fade in to Murder. Koenig was best known as Chekov in the Star Trek franchise. His appearance is an in-joke as the murderer in the episode is William Shatner – Captain Kirk from Star Trek. While he got on with Leonard Nimoy and DeForest Kelly, Shatner said he was shocked to discover decades later that the rest of the cast in Star Trek (especially James Doohan and George Takei) seemed to dislike him and all slagged him off in their books. Walter Koenig always recalled a famous incident where William Shatner introduced the cast for a press event announcing Star Trek: The Motion Picture and when Shatner had to introduce Koenig he couldn't remember his name!

(57) More than one episode of Columbo has been set in a film studio lot. This is a handy way for the production to save money by not going anywhere!

(58) Pat Morita has a small part in Étude in Black. Morita would later play Mr. Miyagi in the Karate Kid movie series.

(59) A Case of Immunity was filmed at Greenacres mansion in Beverly Hills. This is the estate that the comedian Harold Lloyd lived in until his death in 1971. The estate and grounds have been used in other productions - like the action film

Commando with Arnold Schwarzenegger.

(60) The origin of the song/nursery rhyme This Old Man (which Columbo enjoys whistling and humming) is rather vague. The song is believed to have originated in Britain.

(61) Peter Falk enjoyed the running gag in Now You see Him in which Columbo's wife had bought him a new raincoat which he disliked. Columbo kept unsuccessfully trying to lose it. He tears it off at one point and declares that he 'can't think in this coat'!

(62) The house on the water in Dead Weight that belongs to Maj. Gen. Hollister was in real life actually owned by Peter Falk and is located in Newport Beach, California.

(63) Roddy McDowall, who played the villain in Short Fuse, was born in London in 1928 and a successful child actor. His family moved to the United States in 1940 to avoid the Luftwaffe blitz on Britain. McDowall became an American citizen and even served in the U.S Army but he never lost his English accent.

(64) In the episode Columbo Goes to the Guillotine, a framed poster of The Amazing Randi is on Max Dyson's workshop. The Amazing Randi is the late James Randi, a magician who debunked psychics and those who claimed to have special powers. Randi was a particular bugbear for the spoon-bending Uri Geller.

(65) Columbo was popular in eastern European communist nations in the 1970s. A factor in this is that the villains were usually well-heeled and Columbo had a working class persona - so it was perceived as being anti-capitalist.

(66) The lowest rated episode of 'New' Columbo on IMDB is No Time to Die. At the time of writing this episode has a rating of 6.3 out of ten.

(67) No Time to Die was previously the title of a 1958 film produced by (future James Bond producer) Cubby Broccoli. The film was also known as Tank Force. In 2021 the new James Bond film was titled No Time to Die - presumably in tribute to Cubby but maybe because they couldn't think of anything else!

(68) The character of Charlie Cale (Natasha Lyonne) in the Rian Johnson show Poker Face is heavily inspired by Columbo.

(69) In the episode Grand Deceptions we see Columbo has started to wear glasses on occasion to read documents.

(70) Columbo's clothes were supplied by Peter Falk. He purchased the famous raincoat and the crumpled suit. Peter Falk said he acquired Columbo's raincoat in New York. He got caught in a rainstorm and ducked into a store to buy a cheap coat. There was a great joke in The Bye Bye Sky-High I.Q. Murder Case where - just for once in sunny Los Angeles television world - it rained but Columbo's raincoat was away being cleaned!

(71) None of the actors playing the Irish characters in The Conspirators were Irish in real life - which does become apparent at times. Clive Revill (Joe Devlin) is from New Zealand. Jeanette Nolan (Kate O'Connell) is American. Bernard Behrens (George O'Connell) is from England. Michael Horton (Kerry Malone) is American.

(72) Columbo nearly always seems to work alone - which is probably not realistic for a homicide detective. The show

worked much better this way though with the focus firmly on Peter Falk and Columbo.

(73) A poll by the survey site YouGov found that 84% of the British public had heard of Columbo.

(74) Peter Falk planned to make a final episode entitled Columbo's Last Case (aka Hear No Evil) in 2007 but despite a completed script all the networks passed on the project and it never got made. Peter Falk was about to turn 80 at the time and, sadly, his failing health soon became apparent. Speculation about dementia sadly turned out to be the case. In late April 2008, Peter Falk was photographed by paparazzi looking dishevelled and confused in the streets of Beverly Hills. Peter was never seen in public again after this and passed away in 2011.

(75) Columbo's Last Case, which Peter Falk never got to make in the end, was going to feature Columbo's retirement bash as he prepares to leave the police force.

(76) The campus scenes in By Dawn's Early Light were filmed at the Citadel in Charleston, South Carolina. This is a military college which opened in 1842.

(77) There were attempts to bring Columbo back in the early 1980s but these obviously didn't amount to anything. Fans would have to wait until 1989 to see the detective again.

(78) Ruth Gordon, who played Abigail Mitchell in Catch Me If You Can, was the oldest actor to play a murderer in Columbo. She was eighty years old at the time.

(79) By the time she appeared in Columbo there was a fresh wave of interest in Ruth Gordon after her appearance in the

cult 1971 film Harold and Maude. Ruth played a 79 year-old woman who develops a friendship/relationship with an alienated young man named Harold (Bud Cort).

(80) Sal Mineo played Rachman Habib in the Columbo episode A Case of Immunity. Sal Mineo was an actor best remembered for playing John "Plato" Crawford opposite James Dean in the film Rebel Without a Cause. Mineo was twice nominated for the Academy Award for Best Supporting Actor for his roles in Rebel Without a Cause and Exodus. Sal Mineo was a big teen idol in his day and was deluged with fan letters. His career though seemed to fade much faster than anticipated. This is generally felt to have been a consequence of the fact that it was an open secret that Mineo was bisexual and didn't care if anyone knew about it. These days no cares cares about the sexuality of actors but it was - sadly - a different matter in Mineo's day.

His sexuality is alleged to have cost him parts in the end. Mineo was said to be rather baffled when the film roles began to dry up. He auditioned to be in big films like The Godfather but obviously didn't get cast. After a part in Escape from the Planet of the Apes he drifted into television and appeared in shows like Columbo and Hawaii Five-O. Sal Mineo did stage a theatre comeback though and won rave reviews for his work on the stage.

(81) Sadly, on February 12, 1976, Sal Mineo was stabbed to death in the alley behind his West Hollywood apartment building. Sal was returning home at about 11-30 at night after doing some rehearsals for a play he was appearing in. He had just parked his car in the garage when a man with a knife appeared and confronted him. People nearby heard screams and found Sal lying in a pool of blood. The blade had pierced his heart. Because his wallet was still on him the police ruled

out robbery as a motive at first. This was pretty odd because a man was seen running from the scene. It seemed pretty obvious that the man hadn't had time to search Mineo. The police suspected a 'homosexual motivation' (whatever that was supposed to mean) for the murder but this predictably turned out to be a blind alley.

In 1979, a pizza deliveryman named Lionel Ray Williams was sentenced to 57 years in prison for killing Mineo. Williams was a violent robber with a long list of crimes. Williams was pretty dumb because he was in jail at the time and kept boasting to other prisoners that he had killed someone famous. The other prisoners obviously ratted him and it came to light that that Williams was probably the person who had stabbed Sal to death in 1976. I say 'probably' because Williams was black and eyewitnesses that night say they saw a white man running away from the murder scene. Williams, when charged, said he'd never heard of Sal Mineo and had no idea who he was.

The upshot of all of this is that there remains a slight sense of mystery about Sal's death - despite the apparent murderer serving time for the crime.

(82) Columbo appears to be slightly bewildered when a villain gives him an uncut cigar. Rather than use a cutter, Columbo prefers to just the bite the end off!

(83) Voters on the Ranker website have Any Old Port In A Storm in first place when it comes to Columbo episodes.

(84) In the episode An Exercise in Fatality, Milo Janus, played by Robert Conrad, is 53 years old. Conrad was only aged 39 at the time.

(85) Peter Falk described Columbo as having the mind of Sherlock Holmes and the dress sense of a gardener!

(86) Columbo was parodied in Mad magazine as Clodumbo. It was published in the January, 1973 issue and a satire of Columbo's pestering of suspects. The suspect is named Dr Robert Culpable.

(87) In the first episode of the second series of The Office (the original BBC version), David Brent (played by Ricky Gervais) does an impression of Columbo during his (disastrous) speech to new staff.

(88) Peter Falk was twice nominated for an Oscar, appeared in plays for Arthur Miller and Neil Simon, worked with John Cassavetes in the American independent cinema movement of the early seventies, and famously played the grandfather reading the story in the cult favorite The Princess Bride.

(89) Clive Revill's character in The Conspirators refers to 'Londonderry' - which is the second largest city in Northern Ireland. However, an Irish Republican in Northern Ireland would never use the name Londonderry. They would simply call the city Derry.

(90) Columbo was designed to be an old-fashioned and unpretentious sort of character who is completely underestimated by the wealthy criminals he has to investigate.

(91) Jack Cassidy appears in three episodes of Columbo turning in wonderful performances as the villain in Murder by the Book, Publish or Perish and Now You See Him. Jack Cassidy was a singer and actor who won great acclaim for his work on Broadway. He appeared in everything from Hawaii

Five-O to Mission Impossible and was in the movie The Eiger Sanction with Clint Eastwood. Cassidy's larger than life presence and natural charisma always made him enjoyable and polished to watch onscreen. He was a great singer too.

(92) Despite all of his accomplishments, Jack Cassidy ended up becoming most famous for being the father of teen pop sensation and Partridge Family actor David Cassidy. There was a window in time where David Cassidy was probably the biggest teen idol in history. David Cassidy, at the height of his fame, could go anywhere in the world and get instantly mobbed by hordes of screaming teenagers.

(93) Stock footage from Super Bowl I was shown in The Most Crucial Game. This was a 1967 game between the Packers and the Chiefs.

(94) Dean Stockwell stars as murder victim Eric Wagner in The Most Crucial Game and as Lloyd Harrington in Troubled Waters. Stockwell had a long career starting out as child actor. He appeared in many cult shows such as Quantum Leap. David Lynch fans will remember him for Blue Velvet and he also gave a memorable performance in the cult Wim Wenders film Paris, Texas.

(95) Columbo often does not immediately introduce himself as a police detective - allowing people to think he is no one of importance. He then surprises them by showing them his police badge.

(96) Two episodes of Columbo, No Time to Die and Undercover, were based on the 87th Precinct novels by Ed McBain. Ed McBain is a pseudonym of Evan Hunter. Over fifty 87th Precinct novels were written between 1956 and 2005. No Time to Die was based on So Long as You Both Shall Live

(1976) and Undercover was based in Jigsaw (1970). A friend had suggested to Peter Falk that the Ed McBain books would make good stories for Columbo episodes so Peter bought the rights to two of the stories to adapt. The decision to adapt two Ed McBain stories is seen as a mistake by some Columbo fans as No Time to Die and Undercover both have poor reputations and were felt to have deviated from the Columbo formula too much.

(97) By Dawn's Early Light is the only episode of the four Patrick McGoohan appeared in that he did not direct.

(98) Lee J. Cobb was considered for the role of Columbo but was unavailable. Cobb (1911-1976) had a long distinguished career in film, television and on Broadway.

(99) Vincent Price appears as David Lang in Lovely But Lethal - although sadly this is a fairly minor role. Price was an art collector, a gourmet chef, an expert gardener with an incredible cymbidium orchid collection, an author, a lover of museums and galleries, and a more distinguished actor than his more high camp horror duties would sometimes allow, once winning raves for a one man show about Oscar Wilde. In two of his very last films, The Whales of August and Edward Scissorhands, he showed there was a lot more to his acting than chewing the scenery up in a dungeon somewhere. The same year that he appeared in Columbo he was also the star of the cult horror film Theatre of Blood.

(100) In Columbo Likes the Nightlife, Columbo doesn't make an appearance until 30 minutes into the episode.

(101) When the series was brought back in 1989 the new Columbo television network ABC used three Peugeot 403 convertibles cars for Columbo's car. You obviously need back

up cars in case one breaks down.

(102) Columbo's pet pooch is simply named 'Dog'.

(103) Columbo is famous for his love of chilli. The earliest mention of Columbo's favorite dish chili comes from an 1828 journal in which a J. C. Clopper talks about sampling chilli in San Antonio. The actual origin of chilli is usually cited as Mexican/Texan although some sources say it was brought to the 'New World' by the Spanish.

(104) Columbo episodes are stand-alone. This means you can watch them in any order you want.

(105) Peter Sellers wanted $360,000 to play the part of murderer Paul Galesko in Negative Reaction. This was deemed too much so they hired Dick Van Dyke. Not long after this the Pink Panther film franchise was successfully reactivated so the chances of getting Sellers in Columbo became even more remote. Sellers was primarily a comic actor but he was also a terrific straight actor - as he later proved again in the film Being There.

(106) Peter Falk negotiated a $600,000 per episode salary and a producer role when he returned as Columbo in 1989.

(107) In Rest In Peace, Mrs Columbo, the murderer Vivian Dimitri (Helen Shaver) attempts to murder Columbo with poisoned marmalade. Marmalade is a fruit preserve usually eaten on toast for breakfast. It is a slightly acquired taste due to its bitterness.

(108) In 1956, around the time he turned 30, Peter Falk declared that was going to be a full time actor ('You gonna paint your face and make an ass of yourself?' said his father)

and was soon enjoying great success on Broadway - especially in a revival of The Iceman Cometh with Jason Robards.

(109) In the episode A Case of Immunity, a young (and then unknown) Jeff Goldblum is an extra in the crowd demonstrating in the scene outside of the legation.

(110) Peter Falk described Columbo as someone who is very comfortable in his own skin. Columbo enjoys his life and job and doesn't really care what people make of him.

(111) There is some rather unconvincing back projection in Try and Catch Me when Columbo takes a spin in the Rolls-Royce. Back projection was common in films and television in this era.

(112) George Gaynes has two roles in Columbo. Étude in Black as Everett and Any Old Port in a Storm where he played a Frenchman - a wine expert who helps Columbo. Gaynes' most famous role was as Commandant Eric Lassard in the Police Academy comedy film series.

(113) Voters on the Ranker website have No Time to Die in last place when it comes to Columbo episodes.

(114) Columbo is very much a creature of habit and man of modest tastes. If he has a coat or car that he likes he will basically keep it forever rather than buy a new one.

(115) In the episode Try and Catch Me, Columbo mentions that both his parents have passed away.

(116) In 2017, Robby the Robot was sold for S$5,375,000 at an auction by Bonhams Auctioneers in New York - making Robby the most expensive film prop ever sold at auction.

(117) Orson Welles was considered for the part of The Great Santini in Now You See Him but he asked for too much money.

(118) Show creators Richard Levinson and William Link stated that they did not give Columbo a first name and did not intend for him to have one. In the first script of season one a reference to Columbo's first name was removed by them.

(119) Peter Falk was in an episode of the legendary television show The Twilight Zone but sadly for Peter it turned out to be one of the worst episodes. The episode is titled The Mirror and has a Central American dictator named Ramos Clemente (obviously patterned after Castro and played by Peter Falk in a ridiculous fake beard) told by General DeCruz (Will Kuluva) that a magic mirror in his office will reveal the face of his would be assassins. Clemente then constantly sees the image of his colleagues in the mirror (transformed into would be killers with knives) and guns and begins a wave of executions in his paranoid state. He grows unpopular but declares he doesn't care about the people. A priest tells him though that the true enemy is one that leaders never recognise - until it is too late. The Mirror is a preposterous and deadly dull episode that even manages to make the mighty Peter Falk ineffective.

(120) It was reported that Columbo became a very popular thing to watch during the pandemic lockdowns. There were many younger viewers discovering the show for the first time.

(121) Richard Basehart, who played Nicholas Frame in the London set Dagger of the Mind, was American in real life but good at accents. He is best known for the Irwin Allen the television show Voyage to the Bottom of the Sea. Basehart was also the narrator in the 1980s crime adventure show Knight Rider with David Hasselhoff.

(122) Robert Culp wore clothes from his own wardrobe in all of his appearances on Columbo.

(123) Columbo is a sports fan and sometimes tries to listen to a game on the radio.

(124) The pier in A Stitch in Crime where Marcia and Dr. Mayfield go to meet, walk and talk is the Malibu Pier, California.

(125) In the British set Dagger of the Mind the scenes involving actor Wilfrid Hyde-White were filmed in California. He owed money to British tax authorities and so could not work in Britain. It is rather too obvious in this episode that the actors are not always really in England.

(126) The quickest murder in the series is in Suitable for Framing - occurring only about a minute into the episode.

(127) Milo Janus offers Columbo breakfast in An Exercise in Fatality but Columbo is rather bewildered when breakfast turns out to be carrot juice and some vitamin pills. Columbo tells Milo there is something wrong with the orange juice!

(128) Peter Falk once said Any Old Port in a Storm was his personal favorite episode. He praised the performance of Donald Pleasance as the murderer.

(129) Columbo Likes the Nightlife features Matthew Rhys as the villain. Rhys and Peter Falk had previously appeared together in a BBC Television adaptation of The Lost World in 2001. The Lost World had Rhys as the hero.

(130) The lake where murderer Paul Galesko and Alvin Deschler meet in Negative Reaction is the Hollywood

Reservoir, Los Angeles.

(131) Back in 1961, the producers Cubby Broccoli and Harry Saltzman (who had secured the rights to adapt Ian Fleming's popular novels) were quite keen on Patrick McGoohan playing James Bond in the first Bond film Dr No. McGoohan was well known at the time for playing John Drake in the television series Danger Man. McGoohan was not only a competent actor but also a proven leading man (albeit on the small screen rather than cinema) who brought an enjoyably offbeat wit to his parts.

Broccoli and Saltzman were disappointed to learn though that Patrick McGoohan had no interest in the part. "It has an insidious and powerful influence on children," said McGoohan when later asked why he had turned down the chance to be James Bond. "Would you like your son to grow up like James Bond? Since I hold these views strongly as an individual and parent I didn't see how I could contribute to the very things to which I objected."

(132) In the episode Butterfly in Shades of Grey, Fielding Chase's mansion was located at 3469 Cross Creek Rd, Malibu. The house was built in 1983 by Linda Thompson. It had nine bedrooms and eleven bathrooms. A railway linked the garden and house. The house has changed hands several times since it was built and the site has been extensively renovated with the railway removed.

(133) Away from Columbo, Peter Falk said he was offered a small part in The Godfather but turned it down (much to the irritation of his agent) because he felt it was too inconsequential.

(134) For the second season of Columbo executives at NBC

thought it would be a good idea to give Columbo a sidekick. Columbo creators Richard Levinson and William Link had the idea of a dog as a sidekick. Peter Falk chose the basset hound at a dog pound.

(135) The famous singer Little Richard has a cameo in Columbo and the Murder of a Rock Star.

(136) Columbo Goes to College has Columbo as a guest lecturer in a criminology class. He discusses a recent episode's case - from Agenda to Murder - explaining how he matched teeth marks belonging to Oscar Finch on a piece of cheese.

(137) Short Fuse was Peter Falk's least favorite of the first season's episodes.

(138) Ed Asner was initially going to be cast as Colonel Rumford in By Dawn's Early Light but he pulled out and Patrick McGoohan took the role.

(139) In the episode The Most Crucial Game, Valerie Harper enjoys top guest star billing but does not appear until three quarters of the way in the episode.

(140) Columbo's love of chilli is an insight into his character. He likes unpretentious and hearty food.

(141) Columbo has a habit of turning up at crime scenes with a boiled egg for his breakfast. In the episode A Stitch in Crime he contaminates the crime scene with egg shell!

(142) Just One More Thing is the title of Peter Falk's autobiography.

(143) Will Geer plays Dr. Edmund Hiedeman in the episode A

Stitch in Crime. Geer was best known for his role in The Waltons. The Waltons is a much loved TV series about a family in rural Virginia during the Great Depression and World War II. It was created by Earl Hamner Jr and ran from 1972 to 1981. Will Geer, who played Grandpa Walton, was married twice but openly bisexual. Geer was involved in gay and left-wing activism and in the 1930s was in a relationship with activist Harry Hay. Geer was blacklisted in the early 1950s for refusing to testify before the House Committee on Un-American Activities. When Geer died in 1978 it was a great blow to The Waltons as Grandpa was such a beloved character.

(144) Swan Song was originally titled Murder by Starlight.

(145) Columbo has a bit of a sweet tooth and buys ice creams several times in the series.

(146) The concert venue at the start of Swan Song is the Universal Amphitheatre, Universal City, California.

(147) The theatre Frame and Stanhope perform Macbeth in in Dagger of the Mind is the Royal Court Theatre in London. Situated in Sloane Square it is a Grade II listed building. The building opened in 1888.

(149) The character of Columbo first appeared in a 1960 episode of the anthology series The Chevy Mystery Show. The episode was entitled Enough Rope. This was adapted by Richard Levinson and William Link from their short story May I Come In. The story is about a police lieutenant then named Fisher. Bert Freed played Columbo. Freed was a prolific character actor on film and TV.

(150) Columbo's Peugeot 403 car was in production from 1955

to 1966.

(151) For the role of the villain in Negative Reaction, Omar Shariff was asked to play murderer Paul Galesko but Shariff wanted a fee of $100,000.

(152) Before he became an actor, Peter Falk tried to join the CIA but he'd worked as a cook in the Merchant Marine. The Merchant Marine had a left-wing Union that you had to be part of and so the CIA rejected him on these grounds.

(153) The background music in the jewelry store in A Friend in Deed is "The End of a Love Affair" by Edward Redding.

(154) On December 11, 1976, forty-nine year-old Jack Cassidy returned home to his west Hollywood apartment after attending some parties. The parties were presumably early Christmas events as the festive season had nearly arrived. Jack Cassidy was probably a bit drunk after this night on the town and the parties. His apartment took up the top floor of the building he lived in. At around 5am, Jack Cassidy felt asleep on his sofa with a lit cigarette. The consequences of this impromptu snooze were tragic and devastating. The apartment was soon in flames and many firefighters were called out. Friends desperately hoped that Jack wasn't in the apartment at the time of the blaze but sadly this obviously wasn't the case. It was Jack himself who had started the blaze in the first place.

The emergency services found one solitary body in the charred remains of the apartment. The body was burned so badly that Jack Cassidy could only be identified by his dental records and the wedding ring he always wore. Cassidy's face, nose, ears, eyes, and skull were burned beyond recognition and his body was reduced to a charred husk. It was a terribly gruesome scene. The official cause of death was cited as 'Extensive Thermal Burns of Body'. You probably didn't need to be Quincy to have worked that one out. Jack Cassidy was much liked in Hollywood and his strange, sudden, and awful death came as a great shock. Many actors attended his funeral and his ashes were later scattered in the Pacific Ocean.

(155) Columbo is a fan of British fish and chips. He gives them a good review in Dagger Of The Mind.

(156) In 2013 a Writers Guild of America list of the 101 Best Written TV Series included Columbo at 57.

(157) Some interiors and the stage for Now You See Him were filmed at The Magic Castle. The Magic Castle is located in Hollywood and a famous private club for magicians and fans of magic. It is the home of the Academy of Magical Arts. It was built in 1909 in a French chateau style and opened as The Magic Castle in 1963. The club is said to be haunted by the ghost of legendary escape artist Harry Houdini!

(158) Leonard Nimoy, the big guest star in A Stitch in Crime, wrote a memoir in 1975 called I Am Not Spock. He later wrote a second memoir called I Am Spock. I Am Not Spock led to a general perception that Nimoy didn't like Star Trek or playing Spock much. I Am Not Spock had dogged the actor since its publication and he felt the need to set the record straight with a new book - I Am Spock. Nimoy wasted no time in explaining himself and began the new memoir by writing that the title I Am Not Spock was intended to be tongue-in-cheek and that in hindsight it was a mistake to use it. As for the suggestion that he was some pompous character who regarded his most famous role to be somehow beneath him, Nimoy said nothing could be further from the truth. He loved Star Trek and Spock ('The Vulcan was always with me,' he

says of his non-Spock years in between the series and the feature films) and was grateful for the doors it opened.

(159) In 1999, TV Guide magazine ranked Lt. Columbo number seven on a 50 Greatest TV Characters of All Time poll.

(160) John Finnegan was a character actor who made thirteen appearances in the Columbo series. He appears in more episodes than any other supporting cast member. He had a wide variety of roles from season one's Blueprint For Murder to the last episode Columbo likes the Nightlife in 2003. He played various characters such as a workman and garbage collector. He had several parts as a police chief. In later Columbo episodes he played Barney of Barney's Beanery where Columbo ate his chilli. He became close friends with Peter Falk at the Actors Studio in his native New York City.

(161) Tyne Daly appears in two episodes of Columbo - as Dolores McCain in A Bird in the Hand and as Dorothea McNally in Undercover. Daly is a distinguished film, television and theatre actress. The most famous role of Daly's career was in the detective show Cagney & Lacey.

(162) Columbo creator Richard Levinson stated that Columbo's 'one more thing' catchphrase was invented when he and William Link wrote the original stage play. A scene was too short and Columbo had exited the stage too early. Having him say 'one more thing' was an easy way to get him back on the stage and kill some time without reams of new dialogue.

(163) Even though Anne Francis's character is killed after fifteen minutes in A Stitch in Crime she has second billing behind villain Leonard Nimoy.

(164) Some of the main cast of the science fiction film Planet

of the Apes appear in Columbo. Kim Hunter plays Zira in Planet of the Apes. She plays Edna Matthews in Suitable for Framing. Roddy McDowall plays Cornelius in Planet of the Apes. He plays Roger Stanford in Short Fuse. Maurice Evans plays Dr Zaius in Planet of the Apes. He appears in Forgotten Lady as Redmond the Butler. Lou Wagner, was Lucius in Planet of the Apes, appears in the Columbo episode Mind Over Mayhem.

(165) Matthew Rhys and Jennifer Sky, the two main leads (alongside Peter Falk) in Columbo Likes the Nightlife, were both only in their twenties at the time.

(166) Fisher Stevens made his film debut in the cultish 1981 summer camp horror slasher film The Burning. The Burning has some memorable gore effects by the great Tom Savini.

(167) Barbara Colby played the doomed store owner Lilly La Sanka in Murder by the Book. Barbara Colby was an American actress known for her comedic flair and toothy smile. As a young woman she studied acting (which included a spell in Paris) and then won plaudits for her work in the theatre. She made her Broadway debut in 1965. Her first major television break came in Columbo and she went on to appear in a number of television shows which included The Odd Couple, Gunsmoke, and Kung Fu. In 1975, Colby played a prostitute named Sherry Ferris in two episodes of The Mary Tyler Moore Show. Colby was a very good scene stealer and had good comic timing.

Barbara Colby's career seemed to be starting to take off by this point and it didn't seem far-fetched to think that she might soon have her own sitcom or start to pick up parts in movies. Colby was married twice and had homes in New York and Malibu. She had a pretty good life. Colby was into

Vedanta and spirituality. This kept her grounded and down to earth. She also loved psychics and tarot readings. She believed in karma and reincarnation.

(168) On July 24, 1975, Barbara Colby was on her way home after teaching an acting class in Venice, CA. She was with a colleague named James Kiernan. As was their custom, they stopped the car in a parking lot and took a break from the long drive. Apparently, this was a tradition for Colby. She liked to take a break and talk about acting with whoever was with her on the way home. While Colby and her friend chatted, a van approached containing two men. The men shot Colby and Kiernan once and then drove away. It was a random and senseless drive by shooting. The shooters didn't even attempt to rob the victims. One of the bullets had hit Colby in the chest and damaged her lung. She almost instantly died of the injuries. She was only 36 years-old. Kiernan was taken to hospital and managed to give a description of the shooters to the police before he too died of his injuries.

Despite the police having a description of the shooters the murders were never solved and no one was convicted for the deaths of Colby and Kiernan. Some men were arrested but it transpired they had nothing to do with the deaths and so they were set free. It appears that the murders were completely random. The men in question didn't even know they were killing a celebrity. At the time there was a huge spike in these sorts of incidents in Los Angeles with homicides and drive by shootings going through the roof. Colby was just desperately unlucky to be in the wrong place at the wrong time. She shouldn't have stopped in that part of town but then hindsight is a wonderful thing. Colby obviously had no way of knowing that stopping for a break in a car parking lot was going to come at the cost of her life.

Barbara Colby's last role was in a 1976 television movie called The Ashes of Mrs. Reasoner in which she starred with Charles During. Colby was murdered three weeks before this movie aired on television. Colby was cremated and her ashes were scattered in the Pacific Ocean. Celebrities and co-stars like Mary Tyler Moore, Cloris, Ed Asner, and Cloris Leachman attended the funeral service. At the time of her death, Colby was playing Liz Erskine in the sitcom Phyllis - which was a sort of spin-off from The Mary Tyler Moore Show. Liz Torres took over the role after Barbara Colby's sad and tragic death.

(169) Suzanne Pleshette, who featured in Dead Weight, said in an interview that Peter Falk deliberately made production of the episode as difficult as possible (often not turning up - which meant stand-ins had to be used in scenes) because he was in a dispute with the studio at the time. Pleshette said she was so annoyed by this she didn't speak to Peter Falk for a year afterwards despite the fact they had been friends for a long time. To be fair to Peter Falk, some stories say it was the studio who blocked him from coming to work.

(170) The Carsini Winery in Any Old Port in a Storm is the Mirassou Winery in real life. This is situated in San Jose, California.

(171) There are a couple of episodes of Columbo where (if you zoom in and freeze) his police ID identifies him as Frank Columbo. The creators of the show did not (as we have mentioned) regard this to be canon. Viewers can speculate for themselves what Columbo's full name might be because it is supposed to be a mystery.

(172) Columbo or his wife frequently turn out to be big 'fans' of whatever criminal suspect he is investigating. It is ambiguous as to whether Columbo is always sincere about this

or whether he is simply attempting to lull the suspect into a false sense of security.

(173) William Shatner played television detective Ward Fowler in Fade in To Murder. There were a number of in-jokes with Fowler's behaviour on set mirroring Peter Falks's disputes with the makers of Columbo.

(174) A few years after the original Star Trek series ended, William Shatner was sleeping in a camper van while doing a comedy farce in a theatre and laying awake at night wondering how he was going to support his wife and three daughters. He hadn't made any money from Star Trek at all. Shatner says Star Trek was just another job at the time and they were amazed when it became a huge cult thing through reruns in the seventies. He only realised how big it was when he attended a convention several years after it ended and was treated like a pop star. Three years after his first appearance on Columbo the first of the Star Trek feature films was released and Shatner was able to reprise his famous role as Captain Kirk on the big screen.

(175) No Time to Die is an atypical Columbo episode as it does not feature a murder and Columbo never meets the main criminal.

(176) In the episode Troubled Waters, the filming location was a real cruise ship called The Sun Princess.

(177) Columbo's first name was the basis of a legal dispute between a trivia expert and the makers of iconic board game Trivial Pursuit. Trivia encyclopedia author Fred L. Worth placed a number of unique false facts in his books. If they appeared elsewhere then he knew that the fact had been copied. One of his false facts was that Columbo's first name

was Philip. In 1984 a version of Trivial Pursuit was released with this fact as one of the questions. Worth filed a lawsuit demanding $300 million from Trivial Pursuit. Judges denied Worth's claim for compensation though Trivial Pursuit admitted they used encyclopedias such as Worth's for questions. And, for the record, Columbo's first name is not Philip!

(178) Although Columbo often talks about his relatives, No Time to Die is the only episode to feature any of them: his nephew Detective Andy Parma.

(179) Stephen Bochco said that when he was joined the Columbo writing staff he was instructed not to write any 'quirks' or comical eccentricities for the character because Peter Falk would add these things naturally as part of his performance. Peter Falk would improvise a lot of a scene and add ad libs. For example - he would search for something in his coat pockets or ask for a pencil. Columbo would talk about his wife and ramble on about random things to annoy the actor playing the suspect for the purposes of the scene.

(180) Peter Falk said in his autobiography he would often change the scripts he was given - even on films - and rewrite his parts and it used to drive the producers of Columbo in particular mad when he did this in the early days.

(181) In the episode Uneasy Lies the Crown, the impressionist and actor John Roarke plays himself in a poker game. Roarke does impressions of John Wayne, Woody Allen, George Bush, Ronald Reagan, and Jack Nicholson in the episode.

(182) In 2012 a poll for Best in TV: The Greatest TV Shows of Our Time, Columbo was rated number 3 in all time legal or cop shows.

(183) Peter Falk said that the ideas for the professions of murderers came from looking through the yellow pages. One time the yellow pages opened up at magicians. And thus the idea for the magician murderer The Great Santini in Now You See Him came about.

(184) Honor Blackman plays murderer Lillian Stanhope in Dagger of the Mind. Blackman was a respected English actress who appeared in numerous roles utilising her glamorous persona. She played John Steed's assistant Cathy Gale in the cult television show The Avengers. Her most famous role was as the Bond girl Pussy Galore in the James Bond film Goldfinger.

(185) In the episode Uneasy Lies the Crown, Colombo says that he is cold as his raincoat does not have a lining!

(186) George Wendt played the killer in the episode Strange Bedfellows. This episode came only two years after the end of the beloved sitcom Cheers - in which Wendt famously played Norm.

(187) Columbo spanned 34 years in all.

(188) Murder by the Book was ranked sixteenth in a TV Guide poll of the 100 greatest television episodes of all time conducted in 1997.

(189) Roddy McDowall's character in Short Fuse is an amateur photographer who has his own darkroom on the office premises. In real life, McDowall was a keen photographer famous for the photos he took of film and television stars.

(190) Peter Falk apparently didn't like Dagger of the Mind very much. This episode tends not to rank very highly when it

comes to Columbo lists - though it does have its fans.

(191) The Stanford Chemical Plant scenes in Short Fuse were filmed at Union Carbide in Torrance, CA.

(192) Peter Falk said that one of his favorite scenes was the one where Columbo is invited on stage to take part in The Great Santini's magic act in Now You See him.

(193) The young Italian waiter in Mario Murder Under Glass is played by Antony Alda. He was the real-life brother of Alan Alda (who among numerous other roles played Hawkeye Pierce in M*A*S*H). Sadly, Antony died in 2009 aged 52.

(194) Columbo's wife is perhaps the greatest example of the 'unseen character' trope. Other examples of this include Norm's wife in Cheers, the wife of Niles in Frasier, and Captain Mainwaring's wife in the classic British sitcom Dad's Army.

(195) Columbo's wife is on the cruise with him in Troubled Waters but we still never see her!

(196) In the episode Death Lends a Hand, Brimmer offers Columbo a $30,000 salary to leave the police and work for his security firm. That would equate to over $200,000 in today's prices. Brimmer of course has an ulterior motive. He wants Columbo out of the police and off the case.

(197) William Link, the co-creator of the series, wrote a collection of Columbo short stories. The Columbo Collection was published in 2010.

(198) Steven Bochco said the villains in Columbo were generally designed to be arrogant and wealthy to make us root for Columbo all the more.

(199) There are examples of slightly more sympathetic villains in Columbo - like Janet Leigh's terminally ill and deluded actress in Forgotten Lady.

(200) While there are some villains that Columbo clearly despises, the detective seems especially kind and respectful to Donald Pleasence's vineyard owner in Any Old Port in a Storm and Johnny Cash's singer in Swan Song.

(201) Janet Leigh plays an aging film star in Forgotten Lady but she was only about 48 at the time.

(202) Lloyd Bochner plays Mazoor Berozski in the chess themed episode The Most Dangerous Match. Bochner was perhaps best known for appearing in the classic Twilight Zone episode To Serve Man. He was also the father of Hart Bochner - who played Ellis in Die Hard.

(203) The Great Santini (in Now You See Him) is undone by the ribbon on an IBM Selectric typewriter. In the 1970s, computers in the home and office were yet to become commonplace so typewriters were still an essential part of offices. IBM Selectric typewriters were very popular and cornered a large share of the typewriter market in the United States.

(204) Footage from 1947 movie Fiesta was used in A Matter of Honor. The film also starred Ricardo Montalbán as a matdor.

(205) Ian McShane appears as Leland St. John in Rest in Peace, Mrs. Columbo. McShane is perhaps best known these days for the HBO show Deadwood and the John Wick films. People in Britain will always remember him for the 1990s show Lovejoy - which was about the adventures of an antiques dealer who is a bit of a lovable rogue. He also had a stint in the popular soap

opera Dallas.

(206) Among the actors who NBC suggested as guest stars for Columbo (but for whatever reason didn't transpire) were Bill Bixby, James Caan, Jerry Lewis, David Niven, George Segal, Anthony Quinn, and Tony Curtis.

(207) Patrick McGoohan's daughter Catherine appeared alongside her father in the episode Ashes to Ashes.

(208) Héctor Elizondo plays the Arabic diplomat Hassan Salah in A Case of Immunity. In real life Elizondo was born in New York to Puerto Rican parents.

(209) Patrick McGoohan was born in New York to Irish parents. He grew up in England and Ireland. McGoohan moved to the United States in the 1970s.

(210) In the episode Mind Over Mayhem, we see Columbo go to (for him) quite extreme lengths to extract a confession out of Dr. Marshall Cahill. Columbo pretends that Dr Cahill's son is going to be charged with the murder - knowing full well that Cahill won't let his son take the rap and will therefore confess.

(211) There are some remarkable carpets in the homes and buildings Columbo visits in the 1970s episodes! Carpeting was a lot more common in those days. People just tend to have floorboards now.

(212) When the show came back in 1989 there was speculation about Steven Spielberg directing one of the new episodes but this obviously never transpired in the end.

(213) Ross Martin, who plays the killer in Suitable for Framing, was Peter Falk's camp counselor when Peter was

twelve. Martin (who was several years older than Peter Falk) was also an acting mentor to Peter.

(214) Dagger of the Mind and A Matter of Honor both take place outside of Los Angeles and place Columbo in a different environment. It probably isn't a coincidence that these two episodes tend to be ranked quite low among the 1970s Columbo stories by some (though obviously not all) fans.

(215) A Columbo board game was released in 1973. This game tends to go for upward of $30 on eBay. The game has a modest score of 5.6 out of ten on BoardGameGeek.Com.

(216) Peter Falk said he loved Columbo's coat because it was very comfortable and lightweight to wear as a costume.

(217) The talk radio host Fielding Chase in Butterfly in Shades of Gray is sometimes said to be based on Rush Limbaugh. Limbaugh was a conservative political commentator with his own radio and TV show. Rush Limbaugh disputed that Fielding Chase was based on him and said the Columbo producers told him no similarities were intentional.

(218) Louis Jourdan was the last villain guest star who was older than Peter Falk in real life.

(219) Fred Astaire was considered to play the murderer Paul Galesko in Negative Reaction.

(220) Columbo Cries Wolf is the first instance where a pop music song is used - She Drives Me Crazy by Fine Young Cannibals.

(221) Five years after his appearance in Columbo, Louis Jourdan played the villain Kamal Khan in the James Bond film

Octopussy.

(222) Columbo appears to be fond of iced tea.

(223) Despite all the cases he has solved and his remarkable skills as a detective, Columbo is never given a promotion in the series.

(224) Columbo hates guns so much that he avoids the mandatory Los Angeles Police Department marksmanship test for ten straight years. When threatened with suspension if he does not take the test he pays a sergeant $5 to take the test for him!

(225) A number of unique videotape releases of Columbo were available in Japan with distinctive covers.

(226) Dick Van Dyke, who played a villain in Columbo, would later play a brilliant detective himself in the popular series Diagnosis Murder. In the show Dick Van Dyke played a doctor who solves murders with his police officer son (played by Dick's real life son Barry).

(227) Columbo often buys his hot dogs from Arthur who runs a hot dog stand at Travel Town, which is a real place in Griffith Park, Los Angeles.

(228) In the episode Étude in Black, the Maestro's house exterior is the same one used in television series The Fresh Prince of Bel-Air.

(229) The number plate of Columbo's car in the seventies series was 044-APD. When the series returned in 1988, the number plate was 448-DBZ.

(230) The formula of Columo was quite novel because it was the polar opposite of a 'whodunit'? The question is not who did the crime but rather how Columbo will manage to outwit them.

(231) The raincoat Peter Falk wore in the show as Columbo did eventually have to be replaced because it became too tattered in the end.

(232) Peter Falk liked to spend his spare time charcoal-drawing and painting.

(233) The raincoat that Columbo wore was one that the producers had seen Peter Falk wearing in real life. They thought it was perfect for the character and asked him to wear it in the show.

(234) William Link said in an interview with the BBC that Peter Falk was a lot like Columbo in real life so it was a perfect fusion of character and actor.

(235) Columbo likes his hot dogs well done to the point of being charred.

(236) Columbo loves black coffee. Before coffee he is 'up' but not really awake.

(237) An installation ceremony for Peter Falk's star on the Hollywood Walk of Fame took place in 2013 a few years after Peter's passing. Dick Van Dyke was among the actors who attended to pay tribute. Peter was actually awarded the star in 1991 but he was so busy he never got around to arranging an installation ceremony!

(238) Peter Falk as Columbo sometimes has an uncanny

resemblance to the Night Gallery era Rod Serling.

(239) You can buy Columbo coffee mugs and t-shirts on Etsy.

(240) Columbo describes himself as a cream soda type of person. Cream soda is a soft drink designed to taste like ice cream.

(241) Peter Falk said that playing Columbo for so many years did constrict his acting career but he had no regrets because he loved the character so much.

(242) Peter Falk said in 1976 that he would happily play Columbo forever.

(243) Columbo has a bash at transcendental meditation in the rather absurdist Last Salute to the Commodore.

(244) Theodore Bikel, who played the highly intelligent villain in The Bye-Bye Sky High I.Q. Murder Case, was a real-life member of Mensa.

(245) Despite the poise and calmness he could project onscreen, Jack Cassidy was a rather troubled man in private by all accounts and suffered from mental health episodes. Neighbors once found him mowing his front lawn naked in the middle of the day.

(246) Susan Clark, who played Beth Chadwick in Lady in Waiting, is Canadian but she lived and worked in London during an early part of her career. In 1965 she appeared on The Benny Hill Show.

(247) Oscar Beregi appears in The Most Dangerous Match. Beregi did many things but is perhaps best known for his lead

role in two excellent Twilight Zone episodes - Deaths-Head Revisited and The Rip Van Winkle Caper. He was also in the (slightly less celebrated) hour long Twilight Zone episode Mute.

(248) Julie Newmar plays Lisa Chambers in Double Shock. Newmar famously played Catwoman for two seasons on the Batman television show with Adam West.

(249) Peter Falk said it was very deliberate the way that when Columbo turns up at a crime scene he sometimes potters around in the background and is barely noticed. Peter said that he wanted Columbo to be the sort of person who doesn't stand out.

(250) Laurence Harvey, who played the chess villain in The Most Dangerous Match, sadly died of cancer only months after the episode was broadcast.

(251) Last Salute to the Commodore is atypical in that we see Columbo working closely with other police officers. This also happens in Now You See Him.

(252) The opening kaleidoscope images of Las Vegas in A Bird in the Hand were previously used in the Banacek episode A Million the Hard Way.

(253) Claudia Christian, who played Lisa Martin in the 1993 Columbo episode It's All In The Game, would land her most famous role a year later as Commander Susan Ivanova in the cult science fiction show Babylon 5.

(254) Molly Hagan, a prolific film and television actress since the 1980s, appeared in two episodes of 'New' Columbo. She was Ruth Jernigan in Murder, Smoke and Shadows

and Victoria Chase in Butterfly in Shades of Grey.

(255) Bruce Kirby appeared in seven Columbo episodes and had another uncredited cameo in another. He played Sgt. Kramer in four of the episodes. His son Bruno Kirby Jr appeared alongside his father in By Dawn's Early Light. Kirby Jr played one of the military school cadets.

(256) The actress Shera Danese was Peter Falk's second wife and widow. They married in 1977. Shera Danese appeared in the Columbo episodes Fade to Murder, Murder Under Glass, Murder, A Self Portrait, Columbo And The Murder Of A Rock Star, Undercover, and A Trace of Murder.

(257) Michael V. Gazzo played Vittorio Rossi in Murder Under Glass. Gazzo was perhaps best known for his Oscar nominated role as Frank Pentangeli in The Godfather Part II.

(258) An MSN article in 2025 ranked Étude in Black as the best Columbo episode.

(259) In a 2023 Variety article, Columbo was ranked the 85th greatest television show of all time.

(260) Columbo was baffled by fax machines when the show returned in the late 1980s. Fax machines are rarely used today because people have email.

(261) In the 1970s run of Columbo they had a couple of back-up raincoats identical to the one the character wore.

(262) The yacht in Last Salute to the Commodore is an 85 foot super-yacht named the Mojo. It was built in 1969 and celebrities used it for parties and other functions - Barry White's ashes were scattered from it in a ceremony attended

by Michael Jackson. George C. Scott and his wife (Columbo actress) Trish Van Devere chartered the yacht in 1978.

(263) Peter Falk said it was always the plan right from the start that Mrs Columbo would never appear in the show.

(264) The airport in Ransom for a Dead Man is Burbank Airport.

(265) The ice cream soda that Alex Brady makes for Columbo in Murder, Smoke and Mirrors consists of ice cream (obviously!), whipped cream, chocolate syrup, and soda.

(266) Peter Falk made a guest appearance in the 1981 film The Great Muppet Caper. This was the second big screen outing for the Muppets.

(267) Columbo suffers from aviophobia - fear of flying.

(268) Columbo says he struggles with detective novels because they are too complex for him!

(269) Peter Falk's last television role was in the 2004 TV film When Angels Come to Town. The cast also included Katey Sagal - who appeared with Peter in the Columbo episode Candidate for Crime way back in 1973.

(270) SlashFilm.Com ranked A Friend in Deed as the best Columbo episode in a 2024 article.

(271) Peter Falk played himself on The Larry Sanders Show in 1992. The Larry Sanders Show was a highly acclaimed sitcom about a fictional chat show. It starred the late Garry Shandling. Rip Torn was Shandling's main co-star. Torn appeared in the 1991 Columbo episode Death Hits the Jackpot.

(272) Sharon Johansen, who played Miss Dudley in Dagger of the Mind, was Playboy magazine's Playmate of the Month in October 1972.

(273) In the episode A Stitch in Crime, we see Columbo get indigestion after he over-indulges at a buffet laid on by Dr. Barry Mayfield. As he mentions to the doctor, due to his job Columbo often ends up missing breakfast and lunch and has to hurriedly eat at random times!

(274) The artist who did the portrait of Columbo in Murder, a Self Portrait was Jaroslav Gebr. Gebr (1926-2013) was born in (what was then) Czechoslovakia. He worked on many film and television productions as an artist. Gebr did the macabre paintings you see in the pilot episode of Rod Serling's Night Gallery.

(275) In the episode Murder Under Glass, Columbo states that his father was born in Italy.

(276) Columbo often talks about his wife and relatives but we only ever meet one of them. This has led to speculation that Columbo might be inventing some of this family trivia to put the suspect at ease.

(277) Columbo says his wife is an avid reader of newspapers - even enjoying the funeral notices!

(278) The Paradise Cove location where Louise's body is recovered in Murder, a Self Portrait is the same location used for Jim Rockford's house trailer in The Rockford Files.

(279) Peter Falk appeared at the Hay Literary Festival in Wales in 2007. This was not long before he was diagnosed with dementia but despite being a little forgetful he was said to be

on good form at the festival. Peter told the audience that Patrick McGoohan was his favorite villain actor and also that he had resisted attempts to make Columbo wear a 'driving coat' in the show and stood firm on the raincoat.

(280) It was reported in 2021 that a barrister's cat interrupted a virtual hearing for the Old Bailey court in London. The (now famous) cat's name was Columbo and it was named after Peter Falk's detective!

(281) A charcoal painting that Peter Falk did of Columbo sold for $1000 online.

(282) The detective series Monk has often referenced Columbo and clearly takes some inspiration from the show.

(283) It has been said that disagreements between Peter Falk and Universal led the studio to consider hiring another actor to play Columbo in 1971.

(284) A number of vintage detective/police shows (like Hawaii Five-O, Kojak, Dragnet, Magnum etc) have had modern reboots but despite occasional rumblings of speculation it has never happened to Columbo. The main problem with a reboot/remake of Columbo is that it is impossible to imagine anyone other than Peter Falk playing this part. It would be a brave actor indeed who attempted to step into Peter's mighty rumpled Columbo shoes. A modern version of Columbo would presumably be pestering murderous tech billionaires!

(285) Only 504 of Columbo's Peugeot 403 Cabriolet convertible car were made in 1959.

(286) In an article about Columbo, the website Variety said part of the show's appeal is that it suggests wealthy people

are deeply weird!

(287) Though rankings are of course purely subjective, many fans rank Columbo Goes to College as the best of the 'New' Columbo episodes. This episode is especially enjoyable because the two young villains regard Columbo to be a bumbling old fool but learn the hard way that he is actually as sharp as a razor.

(288) Steven Bochco said he thought Columbo sometimes got a bit bloated and meandering in two hour episodes.

(289) In the episode Ashes to Ashes, Columbo says diamonds do not burn. But they do at around 900 °C.

(290) In the episode Murder Under Glass the meal Columbo prepares at the end is veal scallopini. This dish consists of thin slices of veal in a lemon butter sauce. It is usually served with pasta.

(291) In a 2017 article, The Guardian newspaper said Last Salute to the Commodore felt like a 'Columbo-related cheese dream' and called the episode a shark-jumping entry for the series.

(292) There is a rather bizarre scene in Sex & The Married Detective when Columbo, for no apparent reason, plays the tuba!

(293) No Time to Die is unavoidably slightly odd because Columbo is at a relative's wedding and yet no one refers to him by his first name!

(294) The hospital exterior in A Stitch in Crime is really the Sheraton Universal Hotel.

(295) Peter Falk said he never gave much thought to the backstory of Columbo's wife or what she did because he knew she was never going to be in the show.

(296) The jazz club in Étude In Black is also used as the basement of the wax museum in Dagger of The Mind.

(297) There is a bronze statue of Columbo (and his dog) on Falk Miksa Street in Budapest. The statue was by the sculptor Géza Dezső Fekete.

(298) Peter Falk, in character as Columbo, 'roasted' Dean Martin in 1978 on The Dean Martin Celebrity Roast.

(299) The reason why Peter Falk was on bad terms with the studio during Dead Weight was money and that his contract stipulated he could direct an episode in that season - Peter suspected that Universal were trying to get out of that agreement and block him from directing. He did though get to direct Blueprint for Murder - the final episode in the first season.

(300) The K44 supercomputer in Mind Over Mayhem is depicted by a CDC 3800. The CDC 3800 was used to control Air Force satellites from the 1960s onwards.

(301) Dr. Bart Keppel in Double Exposure is largely inspired by James Vicary. Vicary claimed that his subliminal advertising in a 1957 experiment increased sales of popcorn and soda by 57% in a cinema. None of this was really true though and Vicary later admitted as much. The experiment was a fake. The difference is that Double Exposure's plot works on the basis that subliminal advertising is real and effective.

(302) Columbo served in the Korean War.

(303) No Time to Die is atypical in that we see Columbo brandish a gun.

(304) Columbo is originally from New York.

(305) In the episode Mind Over Mayhem the computer room sets were reused from science fiction film The Andromeda Strain.

(306) Columbo co-creator William Link took legal action in the 2010s over 40 years of unpaid Columbo royalties. The general gist of the complaint was that Link and Richard Levinson alleged they were shortchanged by Universal on the profits made by Columbo and this breached contracts they had signed in the early 1970s. The matter was finally settled in 2023 - by which time Link and Levinson had passed away and this dispute had now passed to their heirs. The terms of the deal were not disclosed.

(307) Patrick McGoohan was a very shy man in real life. Peter Falk said that a reluctant McGoohan actually had to be talked into allowing the paperwork to be submitted so that he qualified for an Emmy through his work on Columbo. McGoohan didn't care about awards and things like that.

(308) Peter Falk said in a BBC radio interview that Patrick McGoohan did some extensive uncredited rewrites on Columbo and never asked for any money when he did this. He did it for free. McGoohan did tread on a few toes though. Jeffrey Cava, the writer of the original Murder With Too Many Notes script, was unhappy when McGoohan rewrote his story.

(309) Patrick McGoohan said in an interview that he rewrote most of the script for By Dawn's Early Light. McGoohan said the main change he made was to depict Colonel Lyle C

Rumford not as a 'leering' villain but more as a man who thinks he is right and therefore somehow justified in his actions.

(310) The episode Forgotten Lady features clips from Walking My Baby Back Home. Walking My Baby Back Home is a 1953 film that Janet Leigh starred in.

(311) Columbo, when the need arises, seems to know enough Italian to be able to converse in the language.

(312) The formula of the Columbo is usually called the 'inverted mystery' in that the audience knows right off the bat who the murderer is.

(313) Columbo's suit was one that Peter Falk owned. He darkened it for the show.

(314) Columbo seems to be especially scruffy and wild haired in By Dawn's Early Light. This is done deliberately to heighten the contrast between the detective and the impeccably turned out cadets and staff at the military college.

(315) William Shatner said that, when he appeared in the show, Peter Fall pranked him a few times by taking out his glass eye.

(316) Last Salute to The Commodore ends with Columbo taking to a rowing boat. This somewhat contradicts the general lore that Columbo doesn't like water and boats.

(317) The music playing in the club in Columbo Likes the Nightlife is by The Crystal Method - specifically two songs from their Tweekend album Roll it Up and Wild, Sweet and Cool.

(318) Columbo grew up near Chinatown when he was in New York.

(319) In the 1972 episode Étude in Black it is revealed Columbo's salary as a police detective is $11,000. According to an online inflation calculator this equates to $83,000 in 2025.

(320) France Nuyen, who played Mary Choy in Murder Under Glass, used to be married to Robert Culp.

(321) Blythe Danner was pregnant when she appeared in Étude in Black. The baby she was carrying was the famous actress Gwyneth Paltrow.

(322) Beluga caviar features in Double Exposure. Beluga caviar consists of the eggs of the beluga sturgeon. Beluga caviar is illegal to import in some countries today because the fish is an endangered species.

(323) There is something chintzy, fake and grotesque about the world some of the villains inhabit in the 1970s Columbo episodes. Their opulent bad taste serves as a deliberate contrast to the unpretentious Columbo - who lives firmly in the real world.

(324) The song being sung by Santini's daughter's boyfriend at the start of Now You see Him is the theme song for Charade.

(325) Steven Spielberg said he was eternally grateful to Columbo because it enabled him to get the job of directing the television film Duel.

Based on a short story by Richard Matheson, this 1971 thriller is a tense white knuckle ride. It revolves around meek commuter Dennis Weaver driving his car through lonely desert highways and being menaced, chased, and genuinely terrified by the unseen driver of a huge tanker truck. There is no real explanation for the truck or its shadowy malevolent driver (who we only see a few fleeting glimpses of) becoming so completely obsessed with Weaver but Spielberg uses this simple premise remarkably well and Duel is regarded to be one of the best television films ever made. It almost deserves a big screen and got one too with a theatrical run in Europe. There is a lot of tension in the film as Weaver's car overheats or plays up at the worst possible moments and the grimy tanker truck continues to chase him as doggedly as The Terminator or Michael Myers might. The belching truck becomes a character in the film itself.

(326) Peter Falk's wife Shera Danese made light of appearing in so many Columbo episodes and pointed out that a bit of nepotism was not exactly new or uncommon in the entertainment industry.

(327) The horror sequel Damien: Omen II featured Lee Grant and Robert Foxworth in prominent roles. Grant had already been in Columbo (Ransom for a Dead Man) while Foxworth would later play the villain in the 'New' Columbo episode Grand Deceptions. Omen III: The Final Conflict had a prominent role for Don Gordon - who played Alvin Deschler in the Columbo episode Negative Reaction.

(328) Columbo has a very healthy audience score of 80% on Rotten Tomatoes.

(329) Peter Falk said that Identity Crisis was one of his favorite episodes because he loved the scenes between Columbo and Patrick McGoohan's Nelson Brenner.

(330) Patricia Mattick, who played young Margaret Wilson in

Ransom for a Dead Man, appeared in several television shows and TV movies in the 1970s. She also - rather bizarrely - had an uncredited part in an episode of the cultish Australian series Prisoner: Cell Block H. Patricia sadly died of cancer in 2003.

(331) James B. Sikking had a tiny part as a police officer in Publish or Perish. Sikking would later play Lt. Howard Hunter in the acclaimed 1980s police series Hill Street Blues - which was co-created by Columbo writer Steven Bochco.

(332) In The Bye-Bye Sky High I.Q. Murder Case, Jamie Lee Curtis has a brief speaking part as a waitress who takes umbrage at Columbo bringing a doughnut into a diner. This was one of her early roles and she was eighteen at the time. Shortly after this Columbo appearance she had her breakthrough role as Laurie Strode in John Carpenter's Halloween.

(333) Ray Milland made two appearances on Columbo - Death Lends a Hand and The Greenhouse Jungle. He sports a (unconvincing) toupee in one episode but doesn't in the other.

(334) In the episode How To Dial A Murder, Columbo says he likes playing pool but does not get much time to play. In real Life Peter Falk was said to be a famed pool shark.

(335) Jonathan Demme directed the Columbo episode murder Under Glass. Demme would later directed the Oscar winning serial killer thriller The Silence of the Lambs.

(336) Matthew Rhys said that he was originally supposed to play the villain in Columbo Likes the Nightlife as a cockney from London but Peter Falk liked his Welsh accent and told

him to just use that.

(337) Patrick McGoohan, through his friendship with Peter Falk, managed to attain a generous amount of power and creative freedom when it came to his contributions to the show.

(338) In the episode Étude in Black, John Cassavetes is not terribly convincing when he has to pretend to conduct an orchestra!

(339) Columbo's job means he is often sleep deprived because murderers tend not to keep 9 to 5 hours!

(340) Columbo episodes usually end with the suspect being taken away by the police. We never see what happened to them at their trial or what plea they put in. It could be the case that a few of them got off due to Columbo's evidence not being deemed sufficient!

(341) Rest In Peace, Mrs. Columbo is the only episode to feature voice-over narration.

(342) Patrick McGoohan using the line "Be seeing you" in Identity Crisis is a reference to The Prisoner.

(343) Columbo is an animal lover. He especially loves dogs.

(344) In some episodes Columbo says he has children and in another he says he doesn't. As a consequence of this we don't really know for sure what the situation is regarding children. The mystery was never likely to be cleared up because we never see Columbo at home.

(345) Columbo suggests in the show that his own house is

quite modest - especially compared to the grand mansions of some of the villains he investigates.

(346) In the episode Now You See Him, when he arrives at the crime scene Columbo is carrying his dinner (chicken) in a brown paper bag!

(347) After the death of Lady Boothroyd (the first female Speaker of the House of Commons) at the age of 93, some of her most prized possessions were auctioned off to raise money for charity. It turned out that among her prized possessions was a complete DVD box-set of Columbo.

(348) Billy Connolly plays the murderer Findlay Crawford in the episode Murder With Too Many Notes. Billy Connolly is a popular Scottish comedian and actor.

(349) In the episode How to Dial a Murder, the dogs lick Columbo's face. Peanut butter can be seen on Peter Falk's neck/face which has been used to entice the dogs.

(350) Patrick McGoohan was considered for the part of Dumbledore in the first Harry Potter film. McGoohan was in poor health though at the time and so not a viable option even if he had been interested.

(351) A Gold Derby article in 2024 ranked Negative Reaction as the best Columbo episode.

(352) The filmmaker and actor John Cassavetes advised his friend Peter Falk not to take the part of Columbo because he didn't think doing a television show would be a good career move. It all turned out ok in the end though and Cassavetes even appeared in the show himself.

(353) Sorrell Booke appeared in The Bye-Bye Sky High I.Q. Murder Case and Swan Song. Sorrell would later play Boss Hogg in the popular television show The Dukes of Hazzard.

(354) Peter Falk wanted Patrick McGoohan to play the killer in Murder with Too Many Notes but McGoohan felt it would be unwise if he played the killer yet again and so simply directed the episode.

(355) Matthew Rhys said that on his last day working on Columbo Likes the Nightlife he managed to get a photograph of himself wearing Columbo's coat!

(356) Columbo has an occasional habit of eating food he finds at crime scenes.

(357) We rarely see Columbo in court - though appearing in court would be something that a police detective would have to do as part of their job.

(358) In one of his Columbo novels, author William Harrington has Columbo explaining that he always wears the raincoat because it acts as a filing system, allowing Columbo to carry around notes and documents.

(359) One of the reasons why Peter Falk took the part of Columbo is that he'd been cheated out of a large sum of money by a manager and so needed the cash.

(360) The network stipulated that Columbo Likes the Nightlife should have young co-stars and a more modern atmosphere.

(361) The culinary themed Murder Under Glass features fugu. Fugu is a Japanese delicacy made from pufferfish. Certain parts of the fish contain lethal amounts of tetrodotoxin, a

potent neurotoxin. Because of this, preparing fugu requires a highly trained chef who knows how to safely remove the toxic parts and prepare the fish for consumption.

(362) A Stitch In Crime was originally titled The Specialist.

(363) Peter Falk said he was once shooting a film in a remote part of Ecuador and a group of kids came running over because they recognised him from Columbo.
(364) The chess themed The Most Dangerous Match was inspired by the fact that chess was a very big deal at the time and in the news. A year previously the Bobby Fischer v Boris Spassky match had taken place - a game that remains the most famous chess match of all time.

(365) Peter Falk said in a 1993 interview that he always got a kick out of people doing Columbo impressions.

(366) William Link said that Peter Falk didn't have to audition for the part of Columbo.

(367) Lovely but Lethal was originally going to be called Beauty Is As Beauty Dies.

(368) The moustache of Fielding Chase in Butterfly in Shades of Gray seems to alter from scene to scene!

(369) James Woods was wanted for the villain role in Strange Bedfellows but this obviously never transpired and they got George Wendt.

(370) Peter Falk said that on Columbo they tried to avoid the standard coda to a mystery where the entire plot is explained to the audience at the end.

(371) David Rasche, who played Patrick Kinsley in A Trace of Murder, is perhaps best known for the 1980s police spoof sitcom Sledge Hammer! In more recent years he had a regular role on the HBO show Succession.

(372) Jennifer Sky, who played Vanessa Farrow in Columbo Likes the Nightlife, is a former model. As an actor she is best known for Cleopatra 2525 and also made appearances in (among other things) Buffy the Vampire Slayer and Xena: Warrior Princess. She appears (at the time of writing) to be retired from acting.

(373) Robert Culp appeared in the Mrs. Columbo episode Word Games.

(374) Peter Falk plays Columbo in more straight fashion in Columbo Likes the Nightlife than he had done in some other 'New' Columbo episodes.

(375) Columbo, true to form, still hadn't replaced his car when the show returned in 1989.

(376) Anthony Andrews, who played the villain in Columbo Goes to the Guillotine, is perhaps best known for playing Lord Sebastian Flyte in the miniseries Brideshead Revisited in 1981. He won a Golden Globe and BAFTA for this miniseries.

(377) Patrick Macnee played Captain Gibbon in the Columbo episode Troubled Waters. Macnee did many things (everything from a Bond film to This Is Spinal Tap to appearing in an Oasis music video) but he was best known for the television show The Avengers. The Avengers was about the urbane bowler hatted John Steed (Patrick Macnee) - a government agent for the 'Ministry' who battled various villains in some often bonkers and surreal plots. Steed's

female agent partners in the show were Cathy Gale (Honor Blackman), then Emma Peel (Diana Rigg), and finally Tara King (Linda Thorson). Although Honor Blackman did it all first, it is Diana Rigg as Emma Peel who is most associated with the heyday of the show, her playful banter with Patrick Macnee and leather catsuits making her something of an icon.

(378) Murder with Too Many Notes and Columbo Likes the Nightlife are the only Columbo episodes released in the 21st century.

(379) It is said that Peter Falk had some battles with the studio over creative control on the show in the 1970s. Peter wanted to have approval over the scripts.

(380) In the episode Butterfly in Shades of Grey, we see Columbo order tea with honey (he is hopelessly confused by the honey drizzle dipper!) to stave off a cold. He takes his tea black and likes it piping hot. As the detective rightly points out, there is nothing worse than lukewarm tea.

(381) Columbo is not a fan of decaf coffee. He needs that caffeine to stay awake!

(382) In the episode Negative Reaction, Columbo is mistaken for a homeless person when he visits a food shelter to question a witness!

(383) The radio interviews with the villain Joe Devlin in The Conspirators were filed at the KGIL radio station in San Fernando.

(384) Columbo's raincoat is single breasted and has five buttons.

(385) Kim Cattrall appears as Joanne Nicholls in How to Dial a Murder. She would go on to appear in many films - like Star Trek VI: The Undiscovered Country and Big Trouble in Little China. Her most famous role was as Samantha Jones in television series Sex and the City.

(386) In the episode Sex and the Married Detective, Columbo gives his rather infamous tuba playing demonstration at the Dorothy Chandler Pavilion in the Los Angeles County Music Center.

(387) The water tank escape trick that The Great Santini tries to use as an alibi in Now You see Him was first performed by Houdini in 1911.

(388) Peter Falk said that Columbo pulling random things out of his coat (like gumdrops and boiled eggs) was designed to anticipate the moment when Columbo will pull something out of his coat that proves relevant and important to the case.

(389) Laurence Harvey was in perhaps the most memorable segment of Rod Serling's Night Gallery. This was the segment titled The Caterpillar - which has a kicker of a twist.

(390) Peter Falk said that Columbo sometimes attributing his criminal deductions or information gathering to something he was told by a relative was very deliberate on the part of the character because Columbo didn't want the criminals to believe he was too smart himself. Columbo wanted them to underestimate him.

(391) Henry Mancini's theme from Charade ends Now You see Him.

(392) Short Fuse came about because Universal were delighted

with the success of Columbo and wanted an extra episode.

(393) Lili Haydn, who played the daughter Jenny Columbo in Mrs. Columbo, later became a rock violinist.

(394) An obvious weakness in the plot of A Trace of Murder is that Patrick Kinsley, being with the police himself, should be aware that Columbo is a formidable veteran investigator who has put numerous clever villains away.

(395) Columbo having one eye would probably - in real life - have disqualified him from being a police detective.

(396) One of Columbo's coats was auctioned for charity in 1974 - fetching $1000.

(397) Peter Falk said they were always determined that Columbo shouldn't be 'gritty' or realistic. They wanted the show to be something that anyone of any age could watch and enjoy.

(398) The Most Dangerous Match feels slightly more constrictive than other 70s Columbo episodes due to a lot of the story taking place in a hotel and restaurant.

(399) Peter Falk was resistant to the idea of Columbo having a dog at first but he came around to the idea in the end.

(400) In a 1985 interview, Patrick McGoohan said that Last Salute to the Commodore came about because Columbo was presumed to be coming to an end and so him and Peter Falk decided to do a 'different' type of Columbo episode and have some 'fun'.

(401) The episode Murder Under Glass offers an enjoyably

dated glimpse at 1970s 'high end' cuisine. Among the foods into this episode are galantine of duck with pistachios, mushrooms stuffed with crab and bechamel sauce, eggs in aspic, and fish in jellied sauce.

(402) Peter Falk said in an interview that he never worried about typecasting through his role as Columbo because in the grand scheme of things it wasn't exactly a bad problem to have.

(403) Eddie Albert, who played Major General Martin Hollister in Dead Weight, was a real life war hero. He was awarded the Bronze Star after the invasion of Tarawa 1943.

(404) Peter Falk and John Cassavetes are believed to have done some uncredited directing on Étude in Black.

(405) Jessica Walter played Dr. Margaret Nicholson in Mind Over Mayhem. Walter's later roles included Archer and Arrested Development but she was probably best known for her performance as the crazy woman who stalks Clint Eastwood in the thriller film Play Misty For Me.

(406) Columbo describes his wife in Troubled Waters as being shorter than him and having her hair in a bun.

(407) Peter Falk's full name was Peter Michael Falk.

(408) William Link wrote a play called Columbo Takes the Rap which was performed circa 2007. Norm Boucher played Columbo. Though big things were anticipated for the play it fizzled out very quickly and didn't make it to Broadway. The story had Columbo investigating a murder in the business world of rap music.

(409) By Dawn's Early Light is the only time in the original series where someone asks Columbo what his first name is. Colonel Rumford asks but doesn't get an answer. Columbo says that his wife is the only person who ever uses his first name.

(410) Andrew Stevens, who played Wayne Jennings in Murder in Malibu, tested for the part of Luke Skywalker in Star Wars. It was obviously Mark Hamill who bagged this part in the end.

(411) Vito Scotti, a character actor with a gift for comedy, appeared in five episodes of Columbo playing different characters. He was a Maitre D in Any Old Port In A Storm,

Mr. Chadwick in Candidate For Crime, Mr. Grindell in Swan Song, Thomas Dolan in Negative Reaction, and Salvatore Defonte in Identity Crisis. Scotti's sozzled witness in Negative Reaction was perhaps his finest hour when it comes to Columbo. You can tell that Peter Falk got a kick out of Scotti because he often seems genuinely amused in his scenes with him on the show.

(412) Priscilla Barnes had an uncredited part as a nurse in the Columbo episode A Deadly State of Mind. Barnes later played Felix Leiter's doomed wife in the 1989 James Bond film Licence To Kill.

(413) The voice of the hospital announcer in A Stitch in crime is an uncredited Majel Barrett. Majel Barrett was married to Star Trek creator Gene Roddenberry. She was the voice of the Enterprise computer (and also played Lwaxana Troi) in Star Trek: The Next Generation.

(414) Jamie Lee Curtis said in an interview that Columbo changed her life because the clip of her as the grumpy

waitress in The Bye-Bye Sky High I.Q. Murder Case was shown on The Tonight Show when Peter Falk was a guest and this opened doors and got her recognised.

(415) Jack Nance had an uncredited appearance in Suitable for Framing. Nance was best known for his association with David Lynch - appearing in Eraserhead, Dune, Wild at Heart, Twin Peaks and Lost Highway.

(416) Columbo says he enjoys bowling as a hobby.

(417) Columbo says his car has over 100,000 miles on the clock in Any Old Port in a Storm.

(418) Theresa Goren's beach house in Murder in Malibu is really the same house belonging to Joanna & Charles Clay in the Last Salute to the Commodore.

(419) Peter Falk said he thought people liked Columbo as a character because he was just a 'common' man who was easy to identify with.

(420) Ricardo Montalbán plays the murderer Luís Montoya in A Matter of Honor. Montalban was best known for the television show Fantasy Island and his role as villain Khan in Star Trek II: The Wrath of Khan (a character he reprised from the Space Seed episode of the television show).

(421) Peter Falk was a fan of the tune This Old Man and whistled it during filming Any Old Port in a Storm as an ad-lib. It became a part of the series and Columbo's theme tune.

(422) Los Angeles in the original series is largely depicted as a place of grand mansions, swanky restaurants, private swimming pools, and parks. We rarely see the underbelly of

the city.

(423) William Link said that in reality no police detective would be permitted to dress as shabbily as Columbo!

(424) In the episode The Conspirators, Columbo says he learned to play darts from Sgt Gilhooley at the 12th Precinct.

(425) Fielding Chase in Butterfly in Shades of Grey is about to take a gun out of his car and shoot Columbo before the police officers on bicycles arrive. It's a miracle really that none of the suspects in the show have murdered Columbo!

(426) Bernard Fox made two appearances in Columbo. He was Det. Chief William Durk in Dagger of the Mind and Purser Watkins in Troubled Waters. Fox was a Welsh born actor who had many credits in American television. He also appeared in a number of big films - including The Longest Day, The Mummy, and Titanic.

(427) Peter Falk's contract on Columbo was said to be on a year by year basis rather than long term.

(428) Kristin Bauer van Straten played Suzie Endicott in the Columbo episode Undercover. Kristin Bauer van Straten would become best known for her role as Pamela Swynford De Beaufort in the vampire television series True Blood.

(429) The population of the city of Los Angeles has increased considerably since the 1970s. There is less traffic in the 1970s Columbo episodes than you would get today.

(430) Columbo is rather put off his food in Swan Song when he learns that the delicious chilli he has sampled contains squirrel.

(431) The highest rated episode of 'New' Columbo on the Ranker website is Agenda for Murder - which is (at the time of writing) voted into 25th place overall.

(432) When he arrives at the crime scene in Agenda For Murder, Columbo can't resist sampling the Parmigiano-Reggiano cheese on the desk and indicates he is going to take it home. Parmigiano-Reggiano is an expensive cheese that originates specifically from the regions of Parma, Reggio Emilia, Modena, and parts of Bologna and Mantua.

(433) The sauce that Columbo asks Paul Girard for a recipe to in Murder Under Glass is Soubise sauce. Soubise sauce is basically an onion sauce which is then thickened in the traditional white sauce way.

(434) The Beverly Estate was used as Arthur Kennicutt's home in Death Lends a Hand. This estate used to be known as The Getz House and featured in The Godfather. It sold for $63 million in 2021 so you'd need deep pockets to own this property.

(435) Greystone Mansion in California, which was used in Dagger of the Mind, has featured in many films and television shows. Batman & Robin, Spider-Man, Ghostbusters II, Star Trek Into Darkness, The West Wing and Gilmore Girls are among the productions which have used it as a shooting location.

(436) Robert Butler, who directed Double Shock and Publish or Perish, said that Peter Falk had a lot of creative control on Columbo to the extent that he felt more like a co-director than the sole director.

(437) Joyce Van Patten appears in Negative Reaction (as the

nun at the homeless shelter) and Old Fashioned Murder where she plays the murderer Ruth Lytton. Van Patten appeared in many TV series and also films like The Bad News Bears and St. Elmo's Fire. She was married to Dennis Dugan - who played the policeman Mac in Last Salute to the Commodore.

(438) Columbo would be the key witness in court at the trials of the murderers he catches because in most cases he investigated them alone.

(439) After letting Columbo's hair go silvery grey, Peter Falk appeared to dye his hair brown again when Faye Dunaway was the guest star.

(440) There was never an episode of Columbo where a black actor played the villain. One of the producers said they were wary of depicting an African-American as a criminal. even so, Sammy Davis Jr was apparently always high up on the list of people they courted to play alongside Falk in an episode so they might have made an exception in his case.

(441) Columbo often seems to have dog biscuits in his coat!

(442) Rolls-Royce cars feature in five episodes of the 1970s Columbo. Having a Rolls-Royce was a way to flaunt one's wealth.

(443) In the episode Dagger of the Mind, the London interiors were shot at the Universal studios.

(444) A lot of the 1970s Columbo episodes are said to have gone over budget and over schedule.

(445) Columbo is not a fan of elevators.

(446) William Link said that Peter Falk was locked out of the editing room on the first season of Columbo because he kept trying to assert some creative control over the show.

(447) James Mason was one of the actors considered for the part of Paul Galesko in Negative Reaction.

(448) Columbo Likes the Nightlife is just a regular episode with no special ending because at the time they didn't know it was going to be the last one.

(449) A lot of the more recent police shows tend to be police procedurals - which is the complete opposite of Columbo. This is a possible factor in the modern popularity of Columbo because the police procedural shows can tend to get a bit samey.

(450) Gretchen Corbett, who played the bikini clad Jessica in An Exercise in Fatality, is best known for her role as Beth Davenport in The Rockford files. She was also in the cultish horror film Let's Scare Jessica to Death.

(451) Peter Falk is said to have had his salary doubled in the 1970s when Columbo became a big hit.

(452) Patrick McGoohan seemed quite intent on stretching the formula of Columbo at times. Some of the offbeat humor he put into the stories didn't always come off.

(453) Chili peppers are rich in vitamins A and C and have anti-inflammatory qualities so you could say Columbo's diet is quite healthy!

(454) Peter Falk said he never spent much time in makeup when he played Columbo because the character is supposed to

look a bit rough and tired.

(455) Steven Moffat, who created the television show Sherlock (with Benedict Cumberbatch), said that Columbo is his favorite detective show.

(456) Only 2,030 1959 Peugeot 403 cars were ever made so maybe Columbo is right when he suggests it is a collector's item.

(457) Anne Ramsey had an uncredited bit part in Lovely but Lethal. Ramsey was probably best known for her role as Mama Fratelli in The Goonies.

(458) Clive Revill and Roddy McDowall were both in the 1973 British horror film The Legend of Hell House. This film is quite good fun if you've never seen it.

(459) Columbo has (at the time of writing) an 8.3 score on Metacritic with 86% of the reviews positive.

(460) Columbo was only a little chap. Many of the villains towered over him.

(461) Joanne Linville, who played Vickie Hayward in Candidate for Crime, was best known for playing a Romulan Commander in the Star Trek episode The Enterprise Incident. She also appeared in an episode of Mrs. Columbo.

(462) Jane Greer played Sylvia Danziger in Troubled Waters. Greer was a big film star in her younger years and known for her vampish beauty. One of her last roles was as Vivian Smythe Niles in Twin Peaks.

(463) Peter Falk said that when he finally got his wish to direct

on Columbo the studio got their own back by giving him Blueprint for Murder - on which he spent a lot of time essentially directing on a construction site!

(464) The Conspirators did some filming at Los Angeles Harbor.

(465) Now You See Him was originally titled Quicker Than the Eye in a first draft.

(466) The Columbo production team considered up to thirty different actors for every role in every episode.

(467) In the episode Old Fashioned Murder the Lytton Museum is located at Mount St. Mary's College, Doheny Mansion, Los Angeles.

(468) Columbo's entrance in A Trace of Murder is rather eccentric because he's handing out bananas to everyone!

(469) Laurence Harvey, who played the killer in The Most Dangerous Match, was the father of the late Domino Harvey. Domino Harvey was a British bounty hunter. Her life and experiences inspired the film Domino, released in 2005, which starred Keira Knightley as Domino.

(470) Peter Falk once said that the main reason he did Columbo was that he wasn't being offered films at the time so needed a job.

(471) You can buy some Columbo themed jigsaws online.

(472) Patrick McGoohan was a very reclusive sort of actor and rarely did interviews.

(473) Dick Van Dyke was inspired casting in Negative Reaction because people were not used to seeing him play a villain. Trivia you'll never need - Dick Van Dyke later played the villain Malduke in a 1987 episode of Airwolf. This was the cheapjack soft reboot of Airwolf with Dick's son Barry taking over from Jan Michael Vincent.

(474) In a review of a Blu-Ray collection for the 1989-2003 Columbo episodes, Entertainment Focus singled out Murder in Malibu and No Time to Die as the weakest links. Many fans of the show would doubtless agree with that view.
(475) Peter Falk appeared on The Johnny Carson Show in 1972 wearing his Columbo costume.

(476) G. K. Chesterton's Father Brown was an influence on Columbo. Father Brown is a Roman Catholic priest and amateur detective.

(477) Jack Cassidy's second wife was the Academy Award winning actress Shirley Jones. Shirley Jones became very well known to a new generation through her role as Shirley Partridge in The Partridge Family. This show also starred her real life step-son David Cassidy.

(478) Murder with Too Many Notes was only broadcast three years after it was finished. It would appear the network didn't have much confidence in the quality of the episode or the audience appetite for a new Columbo film.

(479) Matthew Rhys said that when he arrived in Los Angeles to play the villain in Columbo Likes the Nightlife he found that Peter Falk was at the airport to greet him and give him a ride in his car. Matthew said he thought this was a very nice gesture.

(480) In the episode Murder with Too Many Notes, Columbo struggles to recognise the theme tune to Jaws!

(481) Peter Falk said that when he directed Blueprint for Murder he got helpful directing advice from John Cassavetes and Steven Spielberg.

(482) There are some trippy dream sequences in The Most Dangerous Match.

(483) There was more than one dog which played Columbo's dog ('Dog').

(484) Peter Falk said that he didn't do much research for Columbo but he did speak to forensics experts with the LAPD a few times.

(485) William Link said when the show came back they managed to find one of Columbo's cars from the original show in San Diego. Luckily it was still running.

(486) At the end of Blueprint for Murder it appears that Columbo has given up smoking. However, his cigar is back in the next series.

(487) William Link said that Peter Falk didn't even like cigars when they started making Columbo, but he thought the cigar was a great prop for the character.

(488) The end of A Trace of Murder, where Columbo explains how he cracked the case in the eatery, feels suspiciously like padding. We (the audience) don't need this information because we've just sat through the episode!

(489) If one were to offer a defence Kate Mulgrew being in her

early twenties at the time in Mrs. Columbo and yet (intially at least) playing Columbo's wife you could argue that she looks older and just because Mulgrew is that age it doesn't mean Kate Columbo is.

(490) The golf course used in Death Lends a Hand is Hansen Dam Golf Course, Pacoima, Los Angeles.

(491) William Link said that when they were courting Bing Crosby to play Columbo their idea was that Crosby would play the character with a pipe rather than a cigar!

(492) The rave warehouse in Columbo Likes the Nightlife is located at 590 South Santa Fe Avenue, Los Angeles. The warehouse was demolished in 2016.

(493) The horse ranch in Strange Bedfellows is located at Ventura Farms, California.

(494) The gravel voiced Patrick O'Neal played the killer in Blueprint for Murder. O'Neal had many credits in film and television. His film roles included The Stepford Wives and Under Siege.

(495) Oskar Werner plays the killer Harold Van Wick in Playback. Werner was a distinctive looking Austrian actor who had many film and stage roles such as Fahrenheit 451. It is said that Peter Falk went to meet Werner in person to persuade him to be in Columbo.

(496) Peter Falk was a perfectionist on set asking for multiple takes which lasted into the night.

(497) Patrick McGoohan's take on Columbo was apparently that Columbo's eccentric affability was all a calculated act

designed to fool whatever suspect he was pestering.

(498) William Link said that Peter Falk was similar to Columbo in that he was a bit forgetful and liked to wear the same clothes all the time.

(499) Jeremy Irons was the first choice to play (what became) Findlay Crawford in the episode Murder With Too Many Notes. Irons was a busy film actor though and impossible to get.

(500) Patrick McGoohan turned down the part of Simon Templar in the 1960s television series The Saint. It was Roger Moore who took the role in the end.

(501) Columbo Likes the Nightlife is somewhat unrealistic in that Peter Falk is 75 and still playing a homicide detective. The average age of law enforcement officers in the United States at their retirement is 55 in real life.

(502) Peter Falk said the main perks of his Columbo fame were front row seats at the basketball and never having to worry about getting a table at a restaurant.

(503) The episode Undercover has Columbo attacked to the extent he has to go to hospital. This feels like an out of place scene for the show.

(504) Columbo seems to run into the mafia more in 'New' Columbo than he did in the old series.

(505) Blueprint for Murder obviously put Peter Falk off directing because he never directed again.

(506) The episode Short Fuse is somewhat infamous today for

Roddy McDowall's tight trousers - which leave little to the imagination.

(507) Paul Gleason had a small part in the episode Identity Crisis. Gleason did many things but was perhaps known for playing the teacher in the John Hughes film The Breakfast Club.

(508) One of Columbo's cars was sold after the 1970s series ended. When the show returned in the late 1980s the owner lent it back to the people making Columbo.

(509) Columbo says he buys his cigars at the supermarket.

(510) Columbo indicates in An Exercise in Fatality that he likes women with a few curves and wouldn't like his wife to be too thin.

(511) An article in Entertainment Weekly in 2023 ranked Columbo as the second greatest fictional detective of all time. Jessica Fletcher was in first place.

(512) Barry Corbin played Clifford Calvert in A Trace of Murder. Corbin has done many things but is perhaps best known for his roles in Northern Exposure and One Tree Hill. In more recent years he has appeared in Better Call Saul and Yellowstone.

(513) Columbo likes saltine crackers with his chilli.

(514) Laurence Luckinbill played the victim Mark McAndrews in the episode Make Me a Perfect Murder. Laurence Luckinbill's most famous role was as Spock's half-brother Sybok in the 1989 film Star Trek V: The Final Frontier.

(515) Columbo's car is French - as he is apt to mention on occasion.

(516) The construction site in Blueprint for Murder is at 1801 Century Park East, Los Angeles. A modern office tower named Century Park Plaza now sits on this site.

(517) Patrick McGoohan left Britain in the 1970s due to the high tax rates at the time (which sent a lot of British based actors into exile). He briefly moved to Switzerland before settling in California.

(518) It is sometimes reported that George C. Scott made a cameo in the episode Make Me a Perfect Murder. Trish Van Devere, who starred in the episode and was married to George C. Scott, debunked this rumor and said it wasn't true.

(519) Mind Over Mayhem tends not to be ranked that highly by Columbo fans. Some felt that the sci-fi trappings were a bit silly and out of place for the show and it suffered from a weak villain. This of course though is all purely subjective.

(520) Peter Falk said that Columbo's raincoat cost him $15 to purchase. This was in 1967.

(521) Richard Levinson and William Link said that when they were planning Columbo as a regular series NBC complained about having a format where it sometimes takes twenty minutes for the leading man to actually show up in the story.

(522) It would probably be fair to say that the 'New' Columbo episodes post 1989 struggled to attract big names in the way that the 1970s Columbo did. There is a theory that higher production costs in that era compared to the 1970s meant they didn't have a huge amount of money to pay guest stars.

(523) The main reason why NBC dropped Columbo after the 1977–78 season is that they seeking a younger demographic to boost ratings and saw Columbo as a show that appealed to older folk. The great irony here is that Columbo is very popular with young people today.

(524) The climax to Short Fuse features the Palm Springs Aerial Tramway. This tramway opened in 1963 so was still pretty new at the time.

(525) The 1969 made for TV film Night Gallery (which was essentially a pilot for the anthology show hosted by Rod Serling) has a lot of future Columbo connections. Two of the segments are directed by Boris Sagal and Steven Spielberg respectively and the first segment stars Roddy McDowall. The final segment stars Richard Kiley - who played the police chief villain Mark Halperin in the Columbo episode A Friend in Deed.

(526) Columbo alternates between chilli with and without beans for a bit of variety.

(527) Patrick McGoohan's cult show The Prisoner built up a huge fandom. McGoohan was very appreciative of this and remained in contact with the Prisoner's appreciation society to express his gratitude.

(528) It seems somewhat unlikely that a real homicide detective would be allowed to take his dog to work with him!

(529) Elaine May famously described Columbo as an 'ass-backwards Sherlock Holmes'.

(530) Patrick McGoohan retired from acting after the Columbo episode Ashes to Ashes although he did do a little bit of voice

acting.

(531) There seems to be a lot of Columbo fanart on Tumblr these days.

(532) In the episode Rest in Peace, Mrs. Columbo we learn that Columbo is a fan of Gary Cooper, Louis Armstrong and Mark Twain.

(533) Peter Falk said in a 1975 interview that he had a low opinion of television before he did Columbo.

(534) Laurence Harvey was best known for the films Room at the Top and The Manchurian Candidate. Room at the Top earned him an Oscar nomination. The Manchurian Candidate was a 1959 thriller novel written by Richard Condon, later adapted into films in 1962 and 2004. The first and best of these starred starred Frank Sinatra, Laurence Harvey, Angela Lansbury and Janet Leigh. Harvey's Raymond Shaw is perhaps the most effective type of spy - an agent who doesn't realise that he is working at all, having been programmed by the government to carry out their bidding.

(535) The sequence in Murder with Too Many Notes where Columbo and a drunken Gabriel drive home is considered by many to be one of the worst interludes in the 'New' Columbo episodes. The scene is supposed to be amusing but it goes on forever and doesn't really work.

(536) Columbo mentioning in Rest in Peace, Mrs. Columbo that he doesn't have children is not to be taken at face value. The suspect is a threat to his family so if Columbo does have kids he isn't going to want to broadcast this fact.

(537) Columbo's badge identifying him as Frank Columbo in

Grand Deceptions was added by the props department with no approval by anyone. In those days you had smaller Cathode Ray televisions so they maybe just presumed no one would be able to read the badge anyway.

(538) Donald Pleasance appeared in the Mrs. Columbo episode Murder Is a Parlor Game.

(539) Mrs. Columbo, initially at least, features Columbo's dog and mentions his raincoat.

(540) Roddy McDowall was in five Planet of the Apes films. He also played Galen in the 1974 Planet of the Apes television series. McDowall said that Galen was his favorite character to play in the Apes franchise.

(541) The Peugeot 403 stopped being produced five years before Columbo was aired.

(542) Penny Johnson Jerald was in the episode Caution: Murder Can Be Hazardous to Your Health. Penny Johnson Jerald has done many things but is perhaps best known as Kasidy Yates, the love interest of Captain Sisko in Star Trek: Deep Space Nine.

(543) A photograph of Captain Kirk from Star Trek can be glimpsed in a scene in Fade in to Murder.

(544) The rather ostentatious billowy blue shirt that Roddy McDowall wears at one point in Short Fuse was a shirt he also wore as the villain in the original Night Gallery television film.

(545) Steven Spielberg said he was encouraged to be as flamboyant as he wanted on Murder By the Book and throw in

some fancy camera shots because Richard Levinson and William Link wanted Columbo to look like a film rather than just a bog standard television show.

(546) Cooper Redman played Gary Hershberger, one of the murderous students in Columbo Goes to College. David Lynch fans will know Hershberger best for his role as Mike Nelson in Twin Peaks.

(547) Robby the Robot is named MM7 in the episode Mind Over Mayhem.

(548) Patrick McGoohan was said to be a religious man who would refuse to take any roles in things which had sexual content.

(549) Martin Landau, who appeared in Double Shock, was a highly acclaimed actor who later won an Oscar for Ed Wood and plaudits for his role in the Woody Allen film Crimes and Misdemeanors. A few years after his appearance in Columbo he was the lead in the cultishly bizarre British science fiction show Space: 1999.

(550) Columbo was apparently very popular in Iran in the 1970s. Manouchehr Esmaeili dubbed Peter Falk into Persian.

(551) Joe Devlin drives a 1952 Jaguar XK 120 Roadster in The Conspirators. It is somewhat ironic that this IRA gunrunner drives such a quintessentially British car but perhaps this is deliberate misdirection because Devlin likes to pretend he is a man of peace.

(552) Peter Falk said that Forgotten Lady was one of his favorite episodes. He said he really enjoyed working with Janet Leigh.

(553) In a 2023 Gold Derby article, Mrs. Columbo was ranked the seventh worst television spin-off show of all time. In case you were wondering, the top three slots went to AfterMASH, Joey, and Beverly Hills Buntz.

(554) In the episode Publish or Perish, Columbo thinks there has been a mistake when he is charged $6 for chili and the iced tea. The waiter looks at the bill and adjusts it to $6.75 - saying he forgot to add the iced tea! Columbo is obviously used to eating in cheaper places.

(555) Character actor Mike Lally appeared in 25 episodes of Columbo.

(556) Robert Loggia, who played the maître d' in Now You See Him, was a highly acclaimed film actor. His credits included Jagged Edge, Prizzi's Honor, Scarface, and Psycho II. Perhaps his best known roles were as the general in the blockbuster science fiction film Independence Day and as "Feech" La Manna in The Sopranos.

(557) Patrick O'Neal played the killer in Blueprint for Murder and later appeared in a more secondary role in Make Me a Perfect Murder.

(558) Columbo says in the episode murder Under Glass that his wife isn't much of a cook.

(559) They say money is the root of all evil and that is certainly the case in Columbo. A great many of the villains are motivated by greed and career advancement.

(560) In the episode Columbo Cries Wolf, Columbo is investigating the murder of a woman from Los Angeles who did not arrive at a meeting in London. Columbo says he is

investigating the murder for his friend Detective Chief Superintendent Durk of Scotland Yard - who appeared in Dagger of the Mind.

(561) At the end of Last Salute to the Commodore, in reference to smoking, Sgt. Kramer tells Columbo he thought he was going to quit. Columbo tells him 'not yet'. The sutbtext of this conversation is a reference to the speculation (at the time) over this being the last ever Columbo episode.

(562) A Friend in Deed uses stock footage from the French Riviera to depict the location of the funeral home.

(563) The cooking show segment in Double Shock was improvised by Peter Falk and Martin Landau.

(564) The title of Dagger of the Mind comes from a famous soliloquy in Shakespeare's Macbeth.

(565) We learn in the episode Identity Crisis that Columbo's wife is a fan of classical music and Madame Butterfly.

(566) Fred Draper appears in six episodes of Columbo in small roles. He is unique in that he had only a small role as Swanny Swanson in Last Salute to the Commodore but was the murderer.

(567) In the episode Columbo Goes to the Guillotine, Columbo states he's never seen anything like the guillotine trick. But in Now You See Him he goes to a magic shop where the shopkeeper shows him a guillotine trick using a carrot and then Columbo's hand.

(568) American character actor Stephen Elliott appeared in two Columbo episodes - A Deadly State of Mind (where he

plays murder victim) Carl Donner and Grand Deceptions - where he plays General Padget. In both episodes his wife his having an affair with the murderer. Elliott's film roles included Death Wish, Beverly Hills Cop, and Arthur.

(569) Columbo Goes to College is one of the few episodes where Columbo appears before the murder happens.

(570) The $300,000 ransom in The Greenhouse Jungle equates to over two million in today's prices. .

(571) In the episode Death Lends a Hand, Columbo tells Kennicut that he was a tearaway as a kid and he thinks that perhaps he became a police officer to make amends.

(572) A Bird in the Hand is the only episode in which Columbo himself is a witness to a murder he solves.

(573) Columbo says he has been in the force 22 years in Uneasy Lies the Crown. Uneasy Lies the Crown was broadcast 22 years after Prescription: Murder in 1968.

(574) William Shatner later made light of his mustache in Butterfly in Shades of Grey. He said the inconsistency of the mustache was distracting!

(575) The pawnbrokers in Strange Bedfellows where Graham McVeigh buys a gun is located at Sunset Pawnbrokers - 1647 N La Brea Ave, Los Angeles.

(576) Due to the production problems caused by Peter Falk's dispute with the studio, Eddie Albert did not find Dead Weight to be a happy experience. Albert is alleged to have called Peter Falk an 'asshole'.

(577) Alan Arkin and Richard Benjamin were considered for the part of Paul Galesko in Negative Reaction.

(578) It has to be said that the villain Graham McVeigh's bearded disguise in the restaurant in Strange Befellows is not terribly convincing!

(579) William Link and Richard Levinson said it was very deliberate that Columbo takes place in a 'mythical' version of Los Angeles.

(580) In the episode Ashes to Ashes, the exterior for the mortuary was Laury's Restaurant Garden Center and Retail Shop located in Glendale. The area had been closed for a year and contained a big parking lot which was perfect for the scenes of the helicopter taking off and landing.

(581) Murder by the Book is the first episode in which Columbo's famous car appears.

(582) William Shatner said he was thrilled to asked to be in Columbo in 1976 because it was regarded to be a very prestigious show.

(583) Burt Young appears in the episode Undercover. Burt Young was best known for playing Rocky's brother-in-law Paulie in the Rocky franchise. There is a Rocky reference in Undercover.

(584) The original title for Short Fuse was Formula For Murder.

(585) Season six only consisted of three episodes.

(586) Anthony Hopkins was offered a role in Last Salute to the

Commodore but he declined.

(587) At the end of Murder Under Glass, the villain Gerard and Columbo both confess that they don't like each other. It is quite rare for Columbo to tell someone he doesn't like them - though to be fair it was in response to Gerad expressing his dislike of the detective.

(588) When he arrives at the crime scene in Negative Reaction, a police officer mistakes Columbo for a man who has brought his car to the junkyard to be scrapped!

(589) Peter Falk said in a 2005 interview that he never got tired of talking about Columbo and loved playing the character.

(590) The highest rated season of Columbo on IMDB is a three way tie between seasons three, four, and six. In these three seasons the average episode score is 7.7 out of ten.

(591) Peter Falk said in a British radio interview that he thought the success of Columbo was down to the fact that it had fairly broad appeal and wasn't targeting any specific audience. People of all ages and backgrounds in many different countries enjoyed the show.

(592) Columbo visiting the homeless shelter mission in Negative Reaction is one of the rare moments in the 1970s series where we get a look at the underbelly of the city.

(593) In a 1971 review of Murder by the Book, The Baltimore Sun praised Peter Falk's performance and the 'quick and clever' writing and direction.

(594) Columbo began as part of The NBC Mystery Movie show

- sharing with McCloud and McMillan and Wife.

(595) Patrick Bauchau, who played the killer Max Barsini in Murder, A Self Portrait, is a Belgian actor. He is perhaps best known for the television series The Pretender. His film credits include A View To a Kill, Panic Room, Clear and Present Danger and Twin Falls Idaho.

(596) In the first episode of Mrs. Columbo, the absence of Lt. Columbo is explained by him being at a police conference in London.

(597) Peter Falk said in the 1970s that he was happy to play Columbo so long as the scripts stayed 'fresh'.

(598) Alfred Fichet in the 1955 film Les Diaboliques is sometimes cited as an incluence on the character of Columbo. Fichet (played by Charles Vanel) is a retired police officer working as a private detective.

(599) Kate Mulgrew said in a 1979 interview that she'd only ever watched one episode of Columbo when she was cast as the detective's wife in a spin-off show.

(600) In his 1971 review of Murder by the Book in the Minneapolis Star Tribune, the television critic Will Jones said the plot didn't make any sense but it was so much fun to watch it didn't really matter.

(601) Brenda Vaccaro turned down the lead role in Mrs. Columbo before it was offered to Kate Mulgrew.

(602) Rosanna Huffman played Tracy O'Connor in Suitable for Framing. She was married to Columbo co-creator Richard Levinson.

(603) Kate Mulgrew said that Mrs. Columbo had to be rewritten when she was cast because the scripts had a much older woman in mind.

(604) Though not everyone agrees with the analysis, some have suggested there is a streak of sadism in Columbo in the way he tirelessly stalks and pesters suspects and never directly (until the end) reveals how much evidence he has against them!

(605) Peter Falk said in one of his 1970s interviews that he was never interested in being famous and his main motivation was always to simply be a good actor.

(606) Peter Falk said a man once asked him how an episode of Columbo had ended because he'd fallen asleep ten minutes into the show!

(607) Mrs. Columbo fizzled out very quickly. By the third episode the ratings were collapsing fast.

(608) Peter Falk said he watched a little bit of Mrs. Columbo and felt that Kate Mulgrew seemed too refined and well-dressed be Columbo's wife.

(609) The third episode of Mrs. Columbo was replaced by a repeat of Quincy because it wasn't finished on time. Kate Mulgrew complained to the media that she'd had two hours sleep in three days because of all the filming on Mrs. Columbo.

(610) Peter Falk once said that the tight shooting schedules in television productions sometimes made it difficult to make anything of quality. He always hated it if a scene had to be rushed.

(611) According to a 1979 article in American Film, the last (1970s) season of Columbo netted Peter Falk $2 million.

(612) Ted Danson was actually in an episode of Mrs. Columbo. This was a few years before he got the role of Sam Malone in Cheers.

(613) Patrick Bauchau, who played the killer Max Barsini in Murder, A Self Portrait, tested for the role of Captain Jean-Luc Picard in Star Trek: The Next Generation. In the end it was a choice between Bauchau and Patrick Stewart and they obviously went with the latter.

(614) A poll in Britain's Radio Times in 2020 ranked Columbo as the fifth greatest television detective. Sherlock Holmes and Hercule Poirot topped the poll.

(615) Peter Falk said they did their best to make Columbo's famous 'one more thing' moments different. In one episode he delivers the line through a window!

(616) The 1973 Columbo board game somehow avoids showing us Columbo's face (he is seen from behind on the box art). Peter Falk had refused permission for his likeness to be used.

(617) Ian Buchanan, who plays the villain Sean Brantley in Columbo Cries Wolf, was born in Scotland. He has made many appearances in American soap operas but David Lynch fans will know him for his role as Dick Tremayne in Twin Peaks.

(618) Some fans think that Columbo seeming to ogle the women at the pool in Columbo Cries Wolf was rather out of character.

(619) Peter Falk is said to have blocked Danny Kaye from

being considered as a villain in the 1970s series. What he had against Danny Kaye was not clear. It could simply be the case that Peter felt Danny Kaye wouldn't have been right for the part.

(620) In an October, 1971 review of Columbo, the Montreal Gazette said that Peter Falk's 'unrelenting' mumbling as Columbo becomes an 'imposition' on the viewer. That review hasn't aged very well!

(621) Regarding the failure of Columbo's Last Case to find a backer, Charles Engel (who was Executive VP of programming at NBC Universal at the time) told the media in 2007 - "No one wants to buy a movie with an 80-year old lead."

(622) Dead Weight is the first episode to feature a military villain. The other two episodes with military villains are By Dawn's Early Light and Grand Deceptions.

(623) Peter Falk said in a 2007 interview that he still had the original Columbo raincoat and kept it in his bedroom closet.

(624) JoAnna Cameron, who played Lorna McGrath in Negative Reaction, later became best known for her role in the kids superhero show The Secrets of Isis.

(625) Columbo is remarkably kind and patient when the nun mistakes him for a homeless person in Negative Reaction!

(626) William Link said that Jack Cassidy was his favorite villain actor in Columbo. He praised Cassidy for being charismatic without going over the top in his performances.

(627) The villain in Playback has a digital watch. The first commercial digital wristwatch came out in 1972.

(628) Peter Falk as Columbo was dubbed initially by Asao Koike in Japan. Koike sadly died in 1985 and Taro Ishida took over Columbo dubbing duties imitating the style of Koike.

(629) There were four strangulations in Columbo.

(630) Last Salute to the Commodore turns the Columbo formula upside down because the murderer is not known to the audience until late in the story.

(631) The Mirassou Winery used in Any Old Port in a Storm has since been demolished.

(632) Sally Kellerman appeared in the episode Ashes to Ashes. Kellerman was best known for role as Major Margaret "Hot Lips" Houlihan in Robert Altman's film M*A*S*H.

(633) H.B. Haggerty played a masseur in Make Me a Perfect Murder. Haggerty was a professional wrestler and actor who appeared in many televisions shows. H.B stood for 'Hard Boiled'. His real name was Don Stansauk.

(634) Robert Culp, sadly, did not play the villain in any of the 'New' Columbo episodes but he did make a memorable appearance in Columbo Goes to College as the father of Justin (one of the killers in the show). Culp's character in the episode is a rich lawyer who thinks he knows everything. He gives Columbo a patronising lecture on how to solve the case - completely unaware that his son is one of the culprits.

(635) Columbo refers to a previous case for the first time in Double Exposure. When he arrives at the crime scene, he said he missed his dinner as he was working late on the Hayward case (from the episode Candidate for Crime).

(636) We see in A Stitch In Crime that Columo doesn't like hospitals very much but then few people do!

(637) The football game footage in A Bird in the Hand is from a Canadian Football League in Edmonton between Saskatchewan Roughriders and the Edmonton Eskimos.

(638) Carsini has a wine vault with air conditioning in Any Old Port in a Storm. In reality a wealthy and serious wine collector like Carsini would have a wine cellar because wine vaults are less reliable when it comes to storing wine safely.

(639) In the episode Lovely but Lethal, Columbo says that he usually carries a salt shaker in his coat to put salt on his egg!

(640) Peter Falk appeared in The Prisoner of Second Avenue on Broadway in 1972. He said he had a panic attack doing the show and that when he went backstage everyone wanted to talk about Columbo rather than the play. It rather put him off Broadway by all accounts.

(641) Columbo's raincoat was made in Spain by a company called Cortefiel. The company makes designer clothing and since the 1970's only sells its clothes in Europe.

(642) A Trace of Murder was presented as a special episode to mark the 25th anniversary of Columbo. It was aired in 1997, 25 years after the first episode in season one in 1971, and 29 years after the pilot Prescription: Murder in 1968.

(643) One obvious problem with the Columbo episodes which take place outside of Los Angeles is that it does strain credibility somewhat that Columbo always seems to stumble into a murder case wherever he goes.

(644) Troubled Waters guest stars Robert Vaughn and Patrick Macnee appeared together in the 1983 television film The Return of the Man from U.N.C.L.E.

(645) Shera Danese said that Peter Falk wouldn't let her play the murder victim in Columbo and the Murder of a Rock Star because that part would have required her to do a love scene with a young actor.

(646) You can buy a variety of Columbo themed t-shirts online.

(647) Peter Falk often played villains and murderers in his early television roles.

(648) José Ferrer, who played Dr. Marshall Cahill in Mind Over Mayhem, was a Puerto Rican actor and director. He earned an Academy Award for Best Actor for Cyrano de Bergerac (1950). His son, the late Miguel Ferrer, was also a successful actor and appeared in everything from Robocop to Twin Peaks.

(649) The Doberman Pinschers in How to Dial a Murder are conditioned to attack when anyone says 'Rosebud'. This is the last line of the main character in Citizen Kane.

(650) Peter Falk said that when they made Murder By the Book he quickly realised that Steven Spielberg was too good for television and destined for bigger things.

(651) In the episode Identity Crisis, the white lined dark jacket Patrick McGoohan wears at the fair is a reference to the jacket he wore in The Prisoner.

(652) James Read played Dr. Wesley Corman in the dentist themed Columbo episode Uneasy Lies the Crown. Read is best

known for the miniseries North & South and his role as Victor Bennett in the series Charmed. He was also in the Legally Blonde films with Reese Witherspoon.

(653) Robert Walker, who played the son Neil Cahill in Mind Over Mayhem, was a prolific television actor. His most famous roles were in the film Easy Rider (as Jack) and as Charlie Evans in the Star Trek episode Charlie X. Soap fans of a certain vintage might remember him as Harding Devers in Dallas.

(654) Peter Falk seems to be amused and laughing for real in the scene in Last Salute to the Commodore where he's shouting up to the worker at the yard.

(655) A recent WhatCulture article ranked Ransom for a Dead Man as the best Columbo episode.

(656) Columbo is so desperate for coffee at the start of Publish or Perish he drinks it lukewarm at the crime scene.

(657) On the Ranker website, season five of Columbo is actually ranked (on votes) below season ten (which is deep into the 'New' Columbo era and was in fact the swansong). It appears that season five was (in the minds of voters) hobbled by episodes like A Case of Immunity, A Matter of Honor, and Last Salute to the Commodore - none of which one would describe as vintage Columbo stories.

(658) Candidate For Crime is the only episode where the murderer (Jackie Cooper as Nelson Hayward) - as opposed to Columbo - is heard whistling 'This Old Man'.

(659) The delicatessen and scene of the murder in Fade in to Murder is located at 3805 Riverside Dr, Burbank. The building has since been demolished.

(660) Columbo Likes the Nightlife aired on January 30th 2003.

(661) Peter Falk said Columbo had the most famous raincoat in the world. You would probably say that Columbo's only rival when it comes to raincoat fame is Paddington Bear!

(662) The villains in Columbo often tend to take him for a buffon. When they finally realised that Columbo was in fact exaggerating his absent mindedness and clumsiness and was as sharp as a tack when it came to solving murders, it was too late for them.

(663) In the episodes A Case Of Immunity and No Time To Die, Columbo wears a tuxedo with his raincoat.

(664) Peter Falk said that Columbo completely changed his life because his face was suddenly known all over the world.

(665) Columbo says in the episode Murder by the Book that he can make a good omelette.

(666) In 2010 the Columbo stage play Prescription: Murder was revived for a tour of the United Kingdom with Dirk Benedict and later John Guerrasio as Columbo.

(667) Columbo was syndicated across 44 countries.

(668) The food at the homeless shelter which Columbo eats in Negative Reaction is beef stew. Well, that is the 'prevailing theory' at any rate!

(669) Antoinette Bower, who played Frances Galesko in Negative Reaction, is a German born retired British actress who appeared in many American television shows (The Twilight Zone, Star Trek, Ironside, Bonanza etc). Her film

roles include the horror films The Mephisto Waltz, Superbeast, and Prom Night (in which she played the mother of Jamie Lee Curtis).

(670) Episodes of Columbo essentially being television movies rather than standard episodes of television was a format which the BBC show Sherlock also adopted.

(671) Robert Vaughn features in two Columbo episodes - as Hayden Danziger in Troubled Waters and Charles Clay in Last Salute to the Commodore. Vaughn had many credits but was best known as Napoleon Solo in the 1960s spy series The Man from U.N.C.L.E and as Gunman Lee in The Magnificent Seven.

(672) Columbo seems to keep invading people's personal space in Last Salute to the Commodore - which is very out of character.

(673) Dabney Coleman made two appearances on Columbo - in Double Shock he plays Detective Murray. In the later Columbo episode Columbo and the Murder of a Rock Star he played the murderer - arrogant defense lawyer Hugh Creighton. Coleman was a highly regarded character actor who had many roles. He passed away in 2024 at the age of 92. His last appearance was in an episode of Yellowstone.

(674) The episodes Requiem for a Falling Star and It's All in the Game both feature an instance where the murderer tries to alter Columbo's image somewhat when it comes to fashion.

(675) In the episode Playback we see that Columbo has a tape dictaphone rather than a pencil and notebook. This doesn't go too well though as Columbo accidentally records himself talking to his dog!

(676) The voice of Peter Falk as Columbo was dubbed by Gian Piero Albertini for Italian television. After the death of Albertini (after the episode Murder, a Self-Portrait) the dubbing was taken over by Antonio Guidi.

(677) The late Sam Wanamaker directed the Columbo episodes The Bye-Bye Sky High IQ Murder Case and Grand Deceptions. He also directed on Mrs. Columbo. Wanamaker had many credits as an actor. Though an American, he spent a lot of time in Britain and held restore the famous Globe Theatre in London. Sam Wanamaker was the father of actress Zoë Wanamaker.

(678) Peter Falk had a say in who played the villains in Columbo.

(679) Cheryl Annie Paris, who played Marcy Edwards in Columbo and the Murder of a Rock Star, is a former fashion model who studied criminal justice in college. Her second husband was the late actor Ken Kercheval - who was famous for his role as Cliff Barnes in Dallas.

(680) Madeleine Sherwood, who played the secretary Miss Brady in By Dawn's Early Light, was arrested in Alabama in 1963 for participating in a 'freedom' walk which supported the civil rights movement and Martin Luther King Jr.

(681) The producers on Columbo wanted an older actor in the part originally. Peter Falk was barely out of his late thirties when he cast - which was younger than they had intended the character to be.

(682) Columbo's upset stomach at the start of Strange Bedfellows is due to a bad experience with some clams.

(683) Carsini puts his fingers at the top of a wine glass at one point in Any Old Port in a Storm. A true wine connoisseur would never do this because body heat might affect the temperature of the wine.

(684) Columbo mistakes the air conditioning ventilator for a piece of modern art at the gallery in Playback!

(685) Peter Falk is buried at Westwood Memorial Park, Los Angeles.

(686) Columbo says he doesn't go to the police headquarters too often because murders never take place there!

(687) The cruise ship in Troubled Waters was used to film the pilot for The Love Boat.

(688) When he appeared in Columbo Goes to College, Stephen Caffrey had just come off the CBS series Tour of Duty - which followed a platoon of soldiers fighting in Vietnam. Tour of Duty was quite popular in its day.

(689) Peter Falk's right eye was the glass one.

(690) Steven Spielberg described Columbo as his 'film school' and said he learned a lot directing his episode on the show.

(691) Chuck McCann's casting as the projectionist in Double Exposure is something of a meta joke because McCann was in a 1970 comedy film called The Projectionist where he played a projectionist who dreams of being a superhero.

(692) Richard Levinson and William Link said that NBC wanted Columbo have a young police sidekick in the show. Thankfully they resisted this suggestion.

(693) Columbo occasionally gives his dog some ice cream.

(694) Full's Irish Dew, the whiskey that Joe Devlin drinks, appears to be a fictional brand.

(695) Shera Danese is a former Miss Pennsylvania.

(696) Peter Falk's mother was Russian and his father was Polish.

(697) Vera Miles, who played Viveca Scott in Lovely But Lethal, was in Psycho and Psycho II as Lila Loomis.

(698) Faye Dunway won the Outstanding Guest Actress in a Drama Series category at the 46th Annual Primetime Emmy Awards in 1994 for her role in It's All In The Game.

(699) Columbo isn't a golf fan. In real life Peter Falk was a golfer though.

(700) Patrick McGoohan spent a lot of his youth in the city of Sheffield in Yorkshire, England. He was evacuated from the city during the Battle of Britain and later worked in the theatre there.

(701) William Shatner is famous for his strange acting style. The way he keeps stopping in the middle of sentences and emphasising random words. He claims that he never noticed this himself but it's clear that at some point (probably in the 1970s) he became self-aware and played up the image for parody.

(702) Mark Ruffalo seems to be the most oft-mentioned name to play Columbo in any potential reboot. This mostly stems from his role in the period thriller Zodiac.

(703) When he appeared on The Johnny Carson Show in 1972, Peter Falk said he had requested duplicates of Columbo's coat be made because the original one was showing some wear and tear.

(704) Columbo Likes the Nightlife came about because Murder with Too Many Notes got a lot more viewers than the network had expected.

(705) The episode Murder Under Glass features sushi. Sushi was more exotic and less common in the 1970s than it is today.

(706) Billy Connolly said in an interview that he has a picture of him and Peter Falk together on his mantlepiece as a momento of his appearance in Columbo.

(707) Richard Levinson and William Link said they had disagreements with Peter Falk on the first season of Columbo because he had strong views about how to play the character and aspects of the scripts that he didn't like. They said that in the end they realised the results were better if they allowed Peter to develop the character his own way.

(708) Laurence Harvey was born in Lithuania. His real name was Zvi Mosheh Skikne. He lived in South Africa for a time before moving to Britain.

(709) Columbo would not have had much longevity if either of the first two choices Bing Crosby or Lee J. Cobb had been cast because both of them sadly died in the 1970s while the original run of the show was still going.

(710) Kate Mulgrew, who starred in Mrs. Columbo and was initially supposed to be the detective's wife, was only twelve

years-old when Peter Falk first started playing Columbo!

(711) Mickey Spillane (creator of Mike Hammer) played the victim in Publish or Perish.

(712) William Link said the key to the success of Columbo is that Peter Falk was very likeable as the character.

(713) At the end of Now You See Him, notice how Santini takes a last look around the bar and stage before he is taken away. He knows he will never see this place again.

(714) Columbo says he has to write everything down because he has a bad memory.

(715) William Link said that when Bing Crosby turned down the part of Columbo he sent them a nice letter explaining that he was retired and just wanted to relax. The grind of a television show wasn't appealing to Crosby.

(716) Eddie Albert, who played Major General Martin Hollister in Dead Weight, promoted tree planting, conservation, and organic farming in real life.

(717) Blueprint for Murder was tricky to shoot because the crew had to schedule their filming around a real construction site where work was actually going on.

(718) An article on GreatDetectives.Net ranked A Stitch in Crime as the best Columbo episode.

(719) In the episode Candidate for Crime, Columbo says he has another car but his wife uses that one.

(720) The number plate on Columbo's car is sometimes

noticeably askew.

(721) There was apparently not a specific brand used for Columbo's cigar on the show. They changed from time to time.

(722) Peter Falk used to joke that Columbo's dog spent longer in the makeup chair than he did!

(723) Voters on the Ranker website have Columbo in first place when it comes to the best television detective shows.

(724) The villain in Playback is rather ahead of his time because he has extensive CCTV. CCTV is much more commonplace today than it was in the 1970s.

(725) Leslie Nielsen has roles in Lady in Waiting and Identity Crisis. Thanks largely to the film Airplane!, Leslie Nielsen would later forge a whole new 'second' career as a comedy actor. He is best known for the Naked Gun films.

(726) Columbo has much shorter hair in Prescription: Murder than the later episodes.

(727) Due to Peter Falk's disputes with the studio, the conclusion of Dead Weight had a body double standing in for Peter Falk from behind and then Falk's dialogue responses were shot later when he was alone. This is all very noticeable now when you watch the scene.

(728) There was a 2013 television film in Japan called Shinano no Columbo which was about a Japanese detective who has taken on the mannerisms and dress sense of Columbo.

(729) Columbo's tumble down the hill in The Greenhouse

Jungle was apparently not scripted.

(730) Patrick McGoohan was said to be the highest paid actor in Britain when his Danger Man series was a hit in the 1960s.

(731) The inverted detective story (in which the crime and perpetrator is revealed at the start) of the type that the Columbo formula follows was invented by the British author R. Austin Freeman (who died in 1943). Many of Freeman's stories featured a detective named Dr. John Evelyn Thorndyke.

(732) A Matter Of Honor and How To Dial A Murder are rather unique in that animals were used as the murder weapon!

(733) It is rather a shame that the great Vincent Price is in a 1970s Columbo but isn't playing the main villain!

(734) Danny Goldman, who played the photographer in Double Exposure, was the voice of Brainy Smurf in the 1980s Smurfs cartoon.

(735) William Link once said that he thought it might be possible that Columbo's wife and relatives are merely fictions designed to disarm suspects with idle small talk.

(736) Steven Spielberg was only 24 years-old when the Columbo episode he directed was first broadcast.

(737) Katy Sagal said in 2023 that her father Boris Sagal gave her a cameo in Columbo so she would get a SAG (Screen Actors Guild) card. Katy said that at the time she didn't even want to be an actor but it was only years later that she realised her father was looking out for her and had shrewdly opened up a lot of doors in her acting career through putting

her in a tiny part in Columbo.

(738) Richard Levinson and William Link said that a key to Columbo's formula is that the villains have to be arrogant, refined, and rich. The show wouldn't work if Columbo was investigating some ordinary person because the contrast between Columbo and the murderer would be minimised.

(739) Steven Spielberg said that when he directed on Night Gallery the crew were quite hostile to him at times because of his youth but he said this never happened when he directed an episode of Columbo.

(740) Peter Falk said in one of his later interviews that he was very grateful to all the fans that embraced Columbo and made it famous.

(741) Columbo wears some rather smart hush puppies in Prescription: Murder - which is in sharp contrast to the scuffed shoes he later wears.

(742) Patrick McGoohan was in the cult 1981 David Cronenberg film Scanners. This film is about 'scanners' - humans with telekinetic abilities who must battle each other and government agents. It is most famous for the head explosion scene at the start!

(743) Peter Falk described the show Mrs. Columbo as 'disgraceful'. He wasn't happy about that show at all.

(744) Gary Hershberger was 26 years-old when he played the student Cooper in Columbo Goes to College.

(745) The technology in Mind Over Mayhem seems a trifle dated - even for the 1970s!

(746) Richard Levinson and William Link also created Mannix, Murder, She Wrote and Ellery Queen.

(747) The cruise ship used in Troubled Waters capsized off the coast of Thailand in 2016. Sadly, it couldn't be refloated so it was left to its fate.

(748) The decision to use 87th Precinct novels by Ed McBain for Columbo by Peter Falk was not supported by other Columbo production staff. One person who did support the change was Patrick McGoohan.

(749) Columbo seems strangely pally with the mafia in some of the 'New' Columbo episodes!

(750) Stanley Ralph Ross (wrote the teleplay for Any Old Port in a Storm and provided the story for Swan Song) had never watched Columbo before he worked on the show.

(751) William Link said that on Columbo they wanted to eschew all the usual cop show clichés like car chases, street prostitutes, and gun shoot-outs.

(752) An article in Empire Magazine in 2025 ranked Columbo as the 93rd greatest television show of all time. In case you were wondering, it was The Sopranos which took the top spot.

(753) Columbo asks Walter Cunnell how much he paid for his shoes in The Most Crucial Game. This was apparently ad-libbed by Peter Falk.

(754) Peter Falk's headstone reads - 'I'M NOT HERE, I'M HOME WITH SHERA'.

(755) In the episode Troubled Waters, Columbo says he once

got seasick from a motel water bed!

(756) Some of the evidence Columbo gathers to arrest criminals would probably be ruled inadmissible in court because he doesn't always get a warrant.

(757) Columbo handing out bananas at the start of A Trace of Murder would not be permitted in real life because police officers are not supposed to eat at crime scenes.

(758) If he had got a promotion, the next rank up for Columbo would be Captain. We can perhaps presume that Columbo resisted any promotion because it may have taken him out of the field - a place where he is most effective and most happy.

(759) Jeff Yagher played Teddy McVeigh in the 1995 episode Strange Bedfellows. Eighties kids might remember McVeigh in the television series V - which span off from the two miniseries. In the story of V, alien flying saucers descend on Earth and hover over cities. The aliens - who are apparently friendly - reveal themselves and appear to look just like humans. These 'visitors' claim they need minerals to save their dying world and offer to share their technology in return. The nations of Earth agree to this exchange but the aliens begin to exert more and more control, persecuting scientists and controlling the media. When cameraman Mike Donovan (Marc Singer) manages to infiltrate one of the alien ships he makes a shocking discovery. The aliens are reptilians who wear masks to pretend they look like humans. Not only that but they eat small live animals and intend to use the people of Earth as food!

(760) In the episode Negative Reaction, Columbo tells the nun at the shelter that he's had his coat for seven years.

(761) Tom Simcox, who played William Haynes in By Dawn's Early Light, was a prolific television actor in the 60s, 70s, and 80s. Simcox did the fantasy action vehicle television treble by appearing in Airwolf, Knight Rider and Street Hawk!

(762) Columbo Cries Wolf is an unusual episode as the victim is not killed in the first act. Also the planning and murder itself is not shown. Columbo solves a murder that was not a murder as the victim is shown to be alive! Of course the "victim" is then murdered for real and Columbo has to solve that murder.

(763) A decision was made by the creators of Columbo to keep the series non violent. The murders are sanitised and there are no shoot-outs or fistfights.

(764) Most of the Columbo novels have been translated into Japanese. First editions go for high prices.

(765) 38 people were killed by shooting in Columbo.

(766) Martin Sheen appears in Lovely but Lethal. This would have been shortly before Sheen had something of a breakout role in the Terrence Malick film Badlands.

(767) Peter Falk believed that an actor is responsible for finding and putting together his own costume.

(768) Columbo's cigar seems to be more unlit in the post 1989 episodes than it was in the original series.

(769) William Link said Columbo deliberately avoided the 'technical jargon' of other police shows.

(770) The New York Daily News gave Murder by the Book a

positive review on September the 16th, 1971. The reviewer (Kay Gardella) said it was fun to watch the game of cat and mouse between Clumbo and the suspect.

(771) Peter Falk said he always enjoyed the episodes of Columbo which took place in the world of showbusiness.

(772) Peter Fischer and Richard Levinson and William Link were initially supposed to be involved in the spin-off show Mrs. Columbo. They disliked the concept but knew it would happen whether they were involved or not so they decided it might better if they had some creative control over it. Fred Silverman, the boss of NBC, was the driving force behind the spin-off show and obviously wanted to ride on the wave of success created by Columbo. Fischer, Link and Levinson wanted to cast an actress of the same age as Peter Falk and had Maureen Stapleton in mind for the role of Columbo's wife. However, to their dismay, Fred Silverman's suggestions were considerably younger than Peter Falk and seemed to chosen for their looks rather than their suitability for the part.

After the casting of 23 year-old Kate Mulgrew, Fischer, Link and Levinson washed their hands of the project and walked away. Fischer said that Mulgrew was a good actress but 'completely wrong' for the part.

(773) After the cancellation of the spin-off series (by then titled Kate Loves a Mystery rather than Mrs. Columbo), Kate Mulgrew complained in a 1979 interview that her character in the show was ill-defined and changed from week to week.

(774) In the episode A Matter Of Honor, Columbo gets in trouble in Mexico after a car accident. But the police know Columbo from the case in Troubled Waters (involving a

Mexican cruise) and so let him off.

(775) Ginger Rogers and Fred Astaire were courted for lead roles in Forgotten Lady but they were not interested.

(776) The real location for the cosmetic company HQ in Lovely But Lethal is Casa Blanca (aka Moroccan Gem) poolhouse at 851 Sand Point Road, Carpinteria, California.

(777) Columbo sports a rather garish Hawaiian shirt on the cruise in Troubled Waters.

(778) Columbo seems to be quite fond of red wine.

(779) In the episode A Bird In The Hand, Columbo says that his wife always gets him to finish the crossword puzzles she starts.

(780) Columbo's Peugeot 403 was available to buy in red, ivory, yellow, metallic blue, metallic green, light grey, metallic dark grey, and black.

(781) Étude in Black was shown as a 75 minute version in Canada before the final 91 minute version was shown in the US.

(782) Rue McClanahan appears as as Verity Chandler In Ashes to Ashes. McClanahan was an actress and comedian. Her most famous role was as Blanche Devereaux on The Golden Girls.

(783) A long writers strike by the Writers Guild of America from March to August, 1988 delayed the return of Columbo to February 1989.

(784) Columbo Goes to College is the first episode where

Columbo is one of the first to discover the victim (with a group of students he has been lecturing to).

(785) In the episode A Friend in Deed, Columbo is paged over his car's police radio. His call number is revealed as "194".

(786) Gil Melle was one of the first composers to use electronic instruments in his work. He composed on four Columbo episodes. Melle's distinctive work also graced the Rod Serling fronted series Night Gallery.

(787) Columbo is fond of fishing.

(788) Jack Cassidy was once a guest villain in I Spy and had a fight scene with Robert Culp. This was obviously before either of them were in Columbo.

(789) William Shatner said that Peter Falk was the key to the success of Columbo. Shatner said that Peter knew the character of Columbo 'inside-out' and understood what worked in the show and what didn't.

(790) Stephen J. Cannell worked on Columbo as a writer. Double Exposure was a spec script that Cannell submitted. He later created a number of television shows - including The A-Team.

(791) It was Stephen J. Cannell who had the idea of Robert Culp playing a villain in Columbo.

(792) In the episode Columbo Goes To College, Columbo says he is taking medication to lower his cholesterol.

(793) Marcia Wallace is not credited in Lady in Waiting despite having a speaking part during the inquest scene. There may

have been a muddle up during production of the first season as she is credited in Murder by the Book - even though she doesn't appear in it.

(794) A Matter Of Honor was originally titled A Matter of Bravery.

(795) Dead Weight and A Stitch in Crime both had scenes filmed at the Los Angeles Petting Zoo.

(796) Joyce Jillson, who played Joan Stacey in Any Old Port in a Storm, was an astrologer who did syndicated horoscopes in more than 200 papers and magazines.

(797) In a 2023 interview, Kate Mulgrew said she thought Mrs. Columbo was a good show which should have run for longer.

(798) Justin Rowe's family in Columbo Goes to College are so rich they actually have servants!

(799) Kate Read, who played the mother Mrs. Walters in Dead Weight, was a highly regarded Canadian actress. Her film roles included The Andromeda Strain and Atlantic City. She also played Linda Loman in the 1985 television film version of Death of a Salesman. Her co-star was Dustin Hoffman.

(800) After the death of Robert Culp in 2010, many of the obits put their focus on I Spy and then seemed to suggest Culp was in an acting wilderness until later roles in things like The Greatest American Hero and Everyone Loves Raymond. Oddly, some of the obituary pieces seemed to completely forget that Culp made such a big contribution to Columbo!

(801) The Columbo episode Lady in Waiting was the last screen appearance by Jessie Royce Landis (who played Mrs.

Chadwick). Jessie Royce Landis had a long film career and was in To Catch a Thief and North By Northwest for Alfred Hitchcock.

(802) Columbo is often rather baffled by computers in the 'New' Columbo episodes post 1989.

(803) Timothy Carey appears in Dead Weight and Fade In To Murder. In both episodes he runs a restaurant and helps Columbo with his opinions on the cases. Timothy Carey was in films by both Stanley Kubrick and John Cassavetes in his career.

(804) Columbo briefly appears in a circus ringmaster's costume at the end of Murder, Smoke and Shadows when he is nailing the villain. This visual flourish doesn't seem to be especially popular with Columbo fans.

(805) There is a shoe theme (ahem) laced into An Exercise in Fatality. This anticipates the evidence Columbo will use to incriminate the suspect.

(806) The creators of Columbo were more influenced by the traditional English drawing room murder mystery than police shows.

(807) The exterior location for Matilda's Art Gallery in Suitable for Framing is at 653 N. La Cienega Boulevard, West Hollywood.

(808) There were negotiations for more Columbo episodes in 1979. The stumbling block was Peter Falk's insistence on more time to shoot the episodes and bigger budgets.

(809) Bruce Kirby appeared in the following Columbo episodes

- Lovely but Lethal, By Dawn's Early Light, A Deadly State of Mind, Identity Crisis, Last Salute to the Commodore, Make Me a Perfect Murder, Columbo Cries Wolf, Agenda for Murder and Strange Bedfellows.

(810) In the episode Death Lends a Hand, the murderer Brimmer says that 10% of the world's population is ambidextrous. In reality only 1% of people are ambidextrous.

(811) A can of silly string features in the episode Short Fuse. At the time silly string had not actually come out for sale and was yet to be patented.

(812) In the episode Murder Under Glass, Columbo says his wife is studying accounting in night school.

(813) Richard Levinson and William Link won an Emmy for Outstanding Writing for Death Lends a Hand.

(814) A producer on Columbo said that in the early days Peter Falk would try to get access to early copies of the scripts so he could judge their quality. In the end they started locking them up so he couldn't do this.

(815) Columbo Likes the Nightlife was the first (and last) Columbo to be in the widescreen format.

(816) Carlene Watkins is listed the end credits of The Bye-Bye Sky High I.Q. Murder Case as Amy but doesn't actually appear onscreen.

(817) William Link and Richard Levinson said the Columbo format was not easy for new writers on the show. The format essentially requires us to watch Columbo deduce what we (the audience) already know.

(818) Gary Conway played the murder victim Ric Carsini in Any Old Port in a Storm. Conway is perhaps best known for his role as Captain Steve Burton in the Irwin Allen sci-fi show Land of the Giants.

(819) In the episode Ransom for a Dead Man, Margaret is watching the film Double Indemnity when arguing in the kitchen. In Double Indemnity a woman kills her husband to claim an insurance payout.

(820) Columbo struggles to keep up with Milo Janus when they run on the beach in An Exercise in Fatality. The actual beach used in the episode is near Paradise Cove - 28128 Pacific Coast Highway, Malibu.

(821) Oliver Brandt's residence in The Bye-Bye Sky High I.Q. Murder Case is located at 10451 Bellagio Road, Los Angeles. It has since been demolished.

(822) There were no Christmas themed Columbo episodes but there was a Christmas themed Columbo novel in 1972 titled A Christmas Killing. In the story Columbo must solve the murder of a store window dresser.

(823) Patrick McGoohan wrote the dialogue for his character in Idenntity Crisis.

(824) Caution: Murder Can Be Hazardous To Your Health was originally titled Smokescreen.

(825) Ric Carsini is said to be 28 in Any Old Port in a Storm. The actor who played him (Gary Conway) was 37 years-old in real life.

(826) In the episode Strange Bedfellows, Columbo says that his

wife's remedy for an upset stomach is soup made with chicken fat and lentils.

(827) How To Dial A Murder had two alternative titles - The Laurel and Hardy WC Fields Citizen Kane Murder Case and Snips And Snails And Murderer's Tails.

(828) Among the alcoholic beverages we see Columbo drink are bourbon, scotch, beer, sherry, and wine.

(829) McLean Stevenson was on the list of names NBC had in the 1970s as potential guest stars for the show. McLean Stevenson was best known for his role as Lt. Colonel Henry Blake in M*A*S*H.

(830) Ed Begley Jr. appears in two Columbo episodes - How To Dial a Murder as Officer Stein and Undercover as Irving Krutch. Begley was friends with Peter Falk in real life.

(831) The United States Copyright Office maintains a list of works which have been registered for copyright purposes. This list contains a number of proposed Columbo episodes/scripts which never went into production. A 1991 Columbo story was titled The Greatest Night In The History Of Fights - which suggests someone proposed a Columbo episode which revolved around boxing. An unproduced 1998 Columbo story is titled Now You See Him, Now You Don't - which indicates it took place in the world of magic (again).

(832) Although we never see Columbo's wife in Troubled Waters some of the staff on the cruise ship report seeing her so that means she does actually exist and isn't merely a figment of Columbo's imagination!

(833) Ken Franklin's lake house in Murder by the Book is

located at 933 Deer Trail Lane, Big Bear Lake.

(834) Ida Lupino played a murder victim in Swan Song and a non-victim in Short Fuse.

(835) In the episode Rest In Peace Mrs Columbo, we see the detective turn up his nose up at the chilli. His favorite diner has a new cook named Heinrich. Columbo has to buy himself an 'orange pop' to take the taste away.

(836) Columbo is much taken with Devlin's pinball machines in The Conspirators. Columbo says that the pinball machines take him back to his youth.

(837) Uneasy Lies The Crown recycled an old script that had been rejected for Columbo many years ago. Steven Bochco originally wrote this script in 1973 for the third season, but it was not made because Peter Falk felt the villain was not strong enough. It was used for the 1977 McMillan & Wife episode Affair of the Heart. McMillan & Wife was a detective series starring Rock Hudson. It ran from 1971 to 1977 and was part of the NBC Mystery Movie Series with Columbo. One of the poker players (Nancy Walker) in Uneasy Lies The Crown was a cast member of McMillan and Wife and Columbo jokes that she was on that "the Rock Hudson mystery show".

(838) The flight in the mountain range in Ransom for a Dead Man is over the Tehapachi Mountains, California.

(839) Louis Jourdan, who played Paul Gerard in Murder Under Glass, was in the French Resistance during the war.

(840) Columbo is asked about the 'Devlin case' by a student in Columbo Goes to College. This doesn't seem to be a reference to The Conspirators because the details of the case are

different.

(841) In the episode Negative Reaction the driving instructor Mr. Weekly (Larry Storch) finds numerous faults with Columbo's car and driving habits - including having no seat belts. This is a memorable comic scene which seems to have some improvisation from the actors.

(842) The same black BMW 750iL is used in Agenda for Murder and Murder in Malibu.

(843) At the start of It's All in the Game, the water in the fountain outside Lauren Staton's house flows backwards - showing that the shot is being payed backwards.

(844) Columbo sometimes has a pyjama top underneath his raincoat when called out to a murder scene during the night.

(845) British actor and presenter Stephen Fry compared Columbo to the ancient Greek philosopher Socrates in an episode of quiz show QI.

(846) The hotel used for the hotel Columbo stays in during the episode Undercover is the Cameo Hotel in Los Angeles.

(847) Peter Falk said that Columbo's personality and character came from the scripts but he added a few quirks.

(848) In the episode Death Hits The Jackpot, Columbo stumbles into a fancy dress party in the course of his duties and is presumed to have come dressed as an eccentric millionaire!

(849) Peter Falk appeared in some commercials for an Italian supermarket chain in 1985 in which he played a Columbo like

character.

(850) In the episode Columbo Cries Wolf there appears to be a goof because we see a postcard from Milan which has a British stamp.

(851) In some of 1970s episodes it is suggested that Columbo is becoming very famous in police circles because of the cases he has cracked.

(852) Oscar Finch has been a famous defence lawyer in Los Angeles for 20 years in Agenda for Murder and yet he has somehow never encountered Columbo before in any of his cases.

(853) Peter Falk said he purchased Columbo's original raincoat on 57th avenue. Peter said that in 1982 he had an exact duplicate made.

(854) Peter Ustinov was yet another person considered for the part of Paul Galesko in Negative Reaction.

(855) We see the top down on Columbo's car in Short Fuse, Lady in Waiting, The Most Dangerous Match, Last Salute to the Commodore and Columbo and the Murder of a Rock Star.

(856) The scenes where Lauren purchases a tie for Columbo in It's All in the Game were filmed at Westfield Mall 6600 Topanga Canyon Blvd.

(857) In the episode A Friend in Deed the helicopter seen on the night patrol switches between two different models – a Bell 206 Jet Ranger and a Hughes 369.

(858) In the episode Negative Reaction, Columbo is asked to

careful when looking at the ransom note and photo as forensics have yet to examine the items but Columbo then handles it with his bare hands!

(859) The role of Tommy Brown in Swan Song was written with Johnny Cash in mind.

(860) Columbo says in the episode Double Exposure that one of the reasons he likes his job is that he gets to meet some very interesting people.

(861) 3 people were killed by drowning in Columbo.

(862) Robert van Scoyk received an Edgar Allan Poe Award from the Mystery Writers of America for his teleplay for Murder Under Glass.

(863) In the episode The Most Crucial Game, Columbo says that he enjoys relaxing in a hammock while listening to a baseball game.

(864) After the death of William Link, Steven Spielberg paid tribute and said that not only had he learned a lot from Link he also owed him much for giving him a break on Columbo and opening doors up in his career.

(865) Columbo explains his tuba playing antics in Sex And The Married Detective by saying that he learnt to play the instrument in high school as it was usually the only one left and available.

(866) The exterior location used to depict Greenleaf's office in Publish or Perish was the Bank of America's HQ in San Francisco.

(867) The Bye Bye Sky-High I.Q. Murder Case reveals that Columbo is a big fan of playing with model trains.

(868) Columbo says he is a terrible shot when it comes to guns.

(869) The stadium exteriors in The Most Crucial Game are the Los Angeles Memorial Coliseum.

(870) In three episodes of Columbo the murderer is a lawyer - Ransom For A Dead Man, Agenda For Murder and Columbo And The Murder Of A Rock Star.

(871) There is a Japanese Kaiseki dinner with Geishas in Murder Under Glass.

(872) In the episode Make Me a Perfect Murder Columbo is shown how to change reels of tape - despite the fact he was shown how to do this in Double Exposure.

(873) The Conspirators script was intended as a pilot for another series but adapted for a Columbo episode.

(874) Columbo seems to like some ketchup with his chilli.

(875) It takes sixteen minutes for Columbo to appear in Murder by the Book.

(876) In the episode Murder by the Book the murderer Ken Franklin drives a 1968 Mercedes 280 SE convertible.

(877) The reason Richard Levinson and William Link didn't write that many Columbo episodes is that they had other commitments.

(878) Columbo earned 39 Primetime Emmy award nominations.

(879) Steven Spielberg is alleged to have disagreed with the cinematographer Russell L Metty on the lighting for Murder by the Book. Metty wanted a film noir style but Spielberg didn't.

(880) Forgotten Lady is the first episode where we see Columbo in a tuxedo.

(881) We see Columbo enjoying chilli at various diners in the show. There wasn't one consistent place through the series.

(882) The western film set Columbo visits in How to Dial a Murder was located at Colonial Street, Backlot, Universal Studios.

(883) At an auction in New York in 2018 a Jaroslav Gebr portrait of Janet Leigh as Grace Wheeler (from Forgotten Lady) sold for $1375.

(884) Peter Falk said that when it was first suggested to him that Patrick McGoohan would be a good guest star in Columbo he had never heard of The Prisoner or even seen McGoohan act in anything.

(885) Peter Falk said it was the producer Everett Chambers who had the idea of putting Patrick McGoohan in Columbo.

(886) Peter Falk once described Columbo as looking like a 'flood victim'!

(887) The NFL football footage A Bird in the Hand is from a Canadian Football League game. The NFL is strict about letting

people use stock footage in television shows.

(888) Leo Penn directed three episodes of Columbo - Any Old Port in a Storm, The Conspirators and Columbo Goes to the Gullotine. Leon Penn was the father of actors Sean and Chris Penn.

(889) Janet Leigh was best known for her role as Marion Crane in Psycho. The blood washing away in the famous shower scene in Psycho was actually chocolate sauce. Chocolate sauce apparently made rather good fake blood in black and white films.

(890) There is a theory that Last Salute to the Commodore was a deliberate act of sabotage by Peter Falk and McGoohan because Columbo was under threat of cancellation. This theory would suggest then that Last Salute to the Commodore was something akin to a scorched earth policy designed to burn bridges and mock the show. It seems rather unlikely this theory is true because Peter Falk and McGoohan were working actors and loved Columbo. It simply seems to be the case that they wanted to do something radical, surreal, and comedic with the format and character. The end result inevitably didn't turn out to be everyone's cup of tea.

(891) Santini in Now You See Him is really a former SS prison guard who has to keep his real identity a secret. As a lower ranking Nazi it probably would have been easier for him to adopt a fake identity and eventually get out of Germany.

(892) John Finnegan is called Lt. Duffy by characters in A Friend in Deed but the end credits list him as Lt. Dreyer.

(893) The auditorium for Dr Mason's lecture and office in How to Dial a Murder was located at Harmony Gold Theater - 7655

Sunset Blvd.

(894) John Cassavetes was in the classic Roman Polanski horror film Rosemary's Baby. He played the husband of Mia Farrow's Rosemary.

(896) In the episode It's All In The Game, Columbo mentions that the longest he ever worked on a case was 9 years and 4 months.

(897) The picnic and basset hound show in Murder, a Self Portrait was held at Griffith Park, Los Angeles.

(898) In the episodes Columbo Goes To College, Short Fuse and Mind Over Mayhem the killer (or killers) use technology/gadgets to commit murder.

(899) Death Hits the Jackpot features a chimpanzee. The chimp turns out to be a (roundabout) factor Columbo cracking the case.

(900) Robert Culp supplied the voice of Dr. Wallace Breen in the classic video game Half-Life 2. He reprised this role for the expansion Half-Life 2: Episode One.

(901) Columbo Goes to College is somewhat inspired by the real life Leopold and Loeb case. Nathan Leopold Jr. and Richard Loeb were two students who committed an awful murder in 1924. They wanted to show how clever they were by committing the 'perfect crime' but both ended up in prison.

(902) The digital watch worn by the villain Harold in Playback is in reality a National Semiconductor.

(903) Peter Falk said the story for 1993's for It's All In The Game was based on an idea he had way back in 1971.

(904) Greg Evigan, who played Harold McCain in Columbo: A Bird in the Hand, is best known for the television shows B.J. and the Bear and My Two Dads. Horror fans of a certain vintage might remember him in the 1989 underwater monster film DeepStar Six.

(905) Forgotten Lady and It's All in the Game are the only two episodes where Columbo allows a murderer to go free.

(906) In the episode Strange Bedfellows we see Columbo conspire with a mafia boss to terrify the suspect into making a confession. I'm not entirely sure this would be permitted as evidence in the trial!

(907) Raye Birk played the murder victim in A Trace of Murder. Birk has many television and film credits. He had a semi-recurring role in the sitcom Cheers as a mailman who feuds with Cliff Clavin.

(908) In the episode Columbo Goes to College the tips of the main rotor blades of the filming helicopter can be seen at the top of the screen during the opening sequence depicting aerial shots of California.

(909) Perino's Restaurant in Murder Under Glass is located at 4101 Wilshire Boulevard. The building was demolished in 2005 and an apartment block was built on site.

(910) Columbo never had any car chases - which is just as well because his car probably would have fallen to pieces!

(911) Peter Falk said that in his view the best Columbo villains

had an elegance to them which made their interactions with the detective enjoyable.

(912) Columbo takes a few snaps of Tower Bridge in Dagger of the Mind.

(913) Season ten of Columbo is not really a traditional season of television but rather a collection of specials which aired between 1990 and 2003.

(914) The creators of Columbo said they loved the way that Jack Cassidy's characters had a complete contempt for Columbo which was barely disguised by all the poise and wit.

(915) Columbo says in the first episode that his wife gives him a pencil each morning but he always contrives to lose it.

(916) When we see Nelson walk out on his balcony to fire the gun through the glass in Candidate for Crime, the cityscape is a rather obvious background painting.

(917) The Williamson Ranch in Blueprint for Murder is located at Hidden Valley, California.

(918) In the episode Murder, Smoke and Shadows, the secretary of the film director Alex has a IBM PS/2 Model 50/70 computer on her desk.

(919) Dick Van Dyke was cast as the murderer in Negative Reaction only a few days before it began shooting.

(920) Ken Franklin's house in Murder By The Book was also used for Eric Wagner's house in The Most Crucial Game.

(921) Dick Van Dyke turned down the part of Robert Thorn in

The Omen and later regretted it. "My god, that was stupid," he said. "Gregory Peck got the part, but at that time there was a lot of violence in it – people impaled on things. I was pretty puritan at the time, a goody-two-shoes, I felt I'd put myself in a position where the audience trusted me. I turned down several things for that reason – either taste or violence or sex or something."

(922) A Friend in Deed and Columbo goes to College both have a similar twist where Columbo fools the suspects into planting evidence - which then proves their guilt.

(923) Columbo is unusual for a television show in that it only has one regular consistent character. Well, two if you count Columbo's dog!

(924) Don Rickles was considered for the role of Alvin Deschler in Negative Reaction.

(925) Vera Miles uses the line 'she couldn't hurt a fly' in Lovely but Lethal. This is a little reference to Psycho.

(926) Columbo stumbles into a belly dancing class in Try and Catch Me.

(927) Columbo Cries Wolf tries to subvert our expectations in that Columbo, for once, turns out to be mistaken about a murder. He does though redeem himself in the end.

(928) Columbo talks to his wife on the phone at the end of Rest In Peace, Mrs. Columbo.

(929) Peter Falk said he imagined Columbo's house as being somewhat chaotic with relatives coming and going and maybe a few kids running around.

(930) Columbo says in Ashes to Ashes that his wife now makes him go outside to have a cigar.

(931) Jack Smight, who directed Dead Weight, was primarily a director of films rather than television shows. Among the films he directed were Damnation Alley, Midway, Airport 1975 and The Illustrated Man.

(932) Anjanette Comer, who plays Jenifer Welles in Étude in Black, who supposed to be in the Harry Palmer film Funeral in Berlin with Michael Caine but illness forced her to withdraw at the last minute. Her film credits include horror curiosities like The Baby and Blood Feast. She later appeared in television shows like Hotel and Jake and the Fatman.

(933) Edward M. Abroms, who directed The Most Dangerous Match, was primarily an editor. Among the films he worked on as an editor were The Osterman Weekend, Blue Thunder, The Sugarland Express and Street Fighter.

(934) Paul Stewart, who played Clifford Paris in Double Shock, was a friend of Orson Welles and was actually a producer on the War of the Worlds radio adaptation Welles did - which terrified some listeners because they thought it was real!

(935) Columbo has a bash at quoits in Troubled Waters but isn't very good. Quoits is a game which involves throwing rings to land over or near a spike.

(936) Peter Falk said that a big part of the Columbo formula was the humor and comic moments in the script.

(937) Phil Bruns, who played Gene Stafford in An Exercise in Fatality, later played Jerry Seinfeld's dad in an episode of Seinfeld.

(938) In the episode Identity Crisis we learn that Brenner knows what music Columbo's wife likes because he bugged the Columbo house. This obviously proves that Columbo's wife is real and not a figment of his imagination!

(939) Ben Gazzara directed two episodes of Columbo - A Friend in Deed and Troubled Waters. Gazzara, like Peter Falk, was a friend and associate of John Cassavetes.

(940) In the episode Strange Bedfellows, Graham McVeigh meets Columbo & Sgt. Phil Brindle at Crossroad's Cafe, Van Nuys, Los Angeles. The building has now been demolished.

(941) The jewelry auction in Death Hits the Jackpot was held at the Biltmore Hotel, Los Angeles.

(942) The 90 minute episodes of the 1970s Columbo actually have a slightly higher IMDB rating on average than the shorter episodes. This somewhat contradicts the general theory that the shorter episodes were better.

(943) According to voters on the Ranker website, the five worst episodes of Columbo are No Time to Die, Undercover, Last Salute To The Commodore, Murder in Malibu and Columbo Likes the Nightlife. The only inclusion there which comes as a surprise is Columbo Likes the Nightlife.

(944) Patrick McGoohan was consulted by Peter Falk even on Columbo episodes that McGoohan wasn't directly involved in.

(945) In the episode Troubled Waters we see that Columbo has taken his raincoat on the cruise!

(946) John Ashton appeared in the Columbo episode Negative Reaction. Ashton is best known for his role as John Taggart in

the (first, second and fourth) Beverly Hills Cop films.

(947) Peter Falk said that the villains underestimate Columbo because he shuffles in all dishevelled and often seems bemused by the case at first.

(948) Columbo often confides to the suspect he is pestering that he is confused by the case. This is plainly deliberate misdirection on Columbo's part in some instances.

(949) The ever suave George Hamilton played a villain in both eras of Columbo. He was in A Deadly State of Mind and Caution: Murder Can Be Hazardous to Your Health.

(950) Gena Rowlands, who appeared in Playback, was married to John Cassavetes and appeared in many of his films. She was good friends with Peter Falk and had worked with him before.

(951) Trisha Noble, who appeared in Playback, was an Australian singer and actress. She was based in Britain in her early acting career and appeared in the Carry On film Carry On Camping. She later appeared in many American television shows like Buck Rogers in the 25th Century, The Rockford Files and Mrs. Columbo.

(952) Otis Young appears in the episode Identity Crisis. A few years previously Young was in the brilliant cult film The Last Detail with Jack Nicholson. The Last Detail was directed by Hal Ashby from a screenplay by Robert Towne. The film revolves around two US Navy Sailors, Billy Buddusky (Jack Nicholson) and "Mule" Mulhall (Otis Young), who are ordered to escort kleptomaniac sailor Larry Meadows (Randy Quaid) by bus and train to a bleak Naval prison for attempting to steal $40 from his base's polio charity - which just happened to be the Commandant's wife's favourite good cause.

Buddusky and Mulhall intend to deliver Meadows as quickly as possible and grab some time in New York but, during the long, dull journey, the pair start to feel sorry for the timid and unworldly young Meadows and become increasingly troubled by their task. Mindful of the fact Meadows is facing eight long years in a tough military prison for an offence they deem fairly innocuous, and hasn't really lived yet, they decide to stretch the journey out and show him a good time before they reach their grim destination.

(953) In an inverted mystery, the suspense comes from watching the detective piece together the puzzle and see if they can solve the crime before the perpetrator gets away with it.

(954) The title of the first literary detective is often attributed to C. Auguste Dupin, a character created by Edgar Allan Poe.

(955) Columbo's raincoat adds to his appearance of an everyman, making suspects underestimate him.

(956) A homicide detective will sometimes find themselves managing more than one case at the same time. Columbo alludes to this on occasion.

(957) The Peugeot 403 typically featured a 1.5-liter four-cylinder engine, which provided adequate power for its time.

(958) Examples of inverted mysteries besides Columbo include works by authors like Julian Symons and certain Ellery Queen stories.

(959) Richard Levinson and William Link said that when they were planning Columbo as a regular series, NBC (stupidly) suggested that Columbo shouldn't have a wife and that way

he'd be free to have romances in the show!

(960) Columbo has a natural curiosity about the world and seems to enjoy meeting new people. This is a big part of the charm of the character.

(961) In the episode Murder Under Glass the end reveals that Columbo suspected Paul Gerard right from the start. Columbo thought it was odd that Gerard dined with a man who was poisoned and yet never went to the hospital to get himself checked out.

(962) Laurence Harvey's character in The Most Dangerous Match is a fan of horror films. This could possibly be a sly reference to Welcome to Arrow Beach - an obscure horror film that Harvey starred in and directed just before he died. In the film Harvey played a Korean War veteran who has become a cannibal!

(963) A wristwatch website calculated that Columbo wore 17 different watches over the entire course of the series. None of them were too fancy or expensive.

(964) Daniel McDonald, who played the kidnapper Strassa in No Time to Die, appeared in many televisions shows and also worked on Broadway. He sadly died of cancer at the age of 46 in 2007.

(965) Peter Falk said that Patrick McGoohan had a big presence as an actor which was palpable on the set.

(966) Matthew Rhys, who played the villain in in Columbo Likes the Nightlife, later won acclaim for his lead role in the drama series The Americans.

(967) Stephen Bochco said that he got a career boost when Peter Falk won an Emmy for Columbo and mentioned and thanked him (Bochco) in his acceptance speech.

(968) Emperor Hirohito, a big Columbo fan like many in Japan, is said to have asked if he could meet Peter Falk during a trip to the United States in 1975. Peter was busy filming though so this couldn't be arranged.

(969) Levinson and Link originally adapted Columbo into the stage play Prescription: Murder which was first performed at the Curran Theatre in San Francisco in 1962. Oscar-winning character actor Thomas Mitchell in the role of Columbo. Mitchell was 70 years-old at the time. Joseph Cotten was the murderer and Agnes Moorehead the victim. Sadly Thomas Mitchell died of cancer while the play was touring.

(970) Peter Falk's first lead in a television series was in CBS's The Trials of O'Brien. The show ran from 1965 to 1966, for 22 episodes. Falk played a lawyer who defends clients while solving mysteries.

(971) The character played by Louise Fitch in Murder in Malibu is called Mrs. Shannon by the characters. In the credits though Fitch is listed as playing Mrs. Gompertz.

(972) Columbo says in Forgotten Lady that his wife is a good singer and dancer.

(973) Peter Falk said that, in his view, he did his best acting on Columbo playing scenes with Patrick McGoohan.

(974) The producers on Columbo said it wasn't easy to attract writers because it was difficult to come up with a good new idea in the detective/inverted mystery format.

(975) Peter Falk said he was self-conscious about his glass eye when he was younger but it never hindered his acting career.

(976) In the episode Negative Reaction the murderer Paul Galesko drives a Rolls Royce Silver Cloud III.

(977) In the episode Identity Crisis, Patrick McGoohan's character drives a green Citroen SM.

(978) Chuck McCann, who played the projectionist in Double Exposure, was an actor, comedian, puppeteer and television host. He was a prolific voice actor for animated children's shows.

(979) In the episode A Case of Immunity the close up of Habib's license shows his birth date as 1918. This would make him 56 years old. Sal Mineo, who played Rahman, was only 36 years old.

(980) The bar where Columbo meets the students in Columbo Goes to College was the Carriage Inn, Sherman Oaks, Los Angeles.

(981) Undercover is the Columbo episode with the most murders.

(982) A big part of the Columbo formula is that the villain usually tries to construct a clever and elaborate alibi for themselves.

(983) Columbo's car conks out in Forgotten Lady and A Friend In Deed.

(984) Jack Cassidy won two Grammy awards for the musical She Loves Me.

(985) Patrick McGoohan's film roles included Ice Station Zebra, Escape from Alcatraz, Silver Streak, Braveheart, and The Phantom.

(986) Columbo enjoys the beach. He says this in the episode The Greenhouse Jungle.

(987) Columbo says in the episode The Bye Bye Sky-High I.Q. Murder Case that he isn't very good at riddles.

(988) Columbo does some rather embarrassing dancing in the episode No Time to Die.

(989) Betsy Palmer plays Lamarr's wife in Death Hits the Jackpot. Palmer played the mother of Jason Vorhees in the first two Friday the 13th slasher films.

(990) The 1970s Columbo was praised for the way it found a lot of roles for mature women. Ageism is a common complaint in Hollywood but it sometimes only seems to apply to women.

(991) In the scene where the nun mistakes Columbo for a homeless person in Negative Reaction you can see Peter Falk and Joyce Van Patten crack up for a second and laugh at each other.

(992) Vic Tayback played the (rather hairy) artist Sam in Suitable for Framing. The gruff voiced Vic Tayback appeared in everything from the original Star Trek series to TJ Hooker.

(993) Durk says in Dagger of the Mind that Sherlock Holmes was Scotland Yard's most famous detective. Holmes didn't work for the police though. He was a private consulting detective

(994) The 90 minute Columbo episodes came about because NBC wanted longer episodes to get more advertising revenue from commercials.

(995) When he gives his lecture in Columbo Goes to College to the students, Columbo says that a good detective always needs some luck.

(996) The first seven seasons were shot on 35 mm film.

(997) The inverted mystery format is sometimes called a 'howcatchem' in that it is a flip reverse of the whodunit.

(998) Peter Falk said that he never stopped getting fan mail for Columbo.

(999) Columbo indicates in The Bye Bye Sky-High I.Q. Murder Case that his wife would like to burn his raincoat!

(1000) Most fans of Columbo would agree that this was the perfect marriage of actor and character. It is impossible to imagine that anyone could have played Columbo so memorably as Peter Falk did.

Photo Credit

https://commons.wikimedia.org/wiki/File:Portrait_Peter_Fal
k_2000.jpg

2000

Stéphane Lemarchand Caricaturiste